INSIDE-OUT
LEADERSHIP

PRAISE FOR THE BOOK

'In an era when time cycles are shrinking for everything, from product life cycles to tenures of CEOs, how do you become, and remain, an enduring and relevant leader? Rajiv, based on his learnings from coaching numerous CEOs, across geographies, spells out a clearly articulated methodology for evolving into a truly respected leader. The secret sauce is to understand yourself and be comfortable with what you see, before venturing out to lead others.'

—Deepak Satwalekar, Independent Director, Wipro, Asian Paints, Piramal Enterprises; Former MD, HDFC and then MD & CEO, HDFC Standard Life Insurance

'Pause . . . reflect . . . reorient. That's what Rajiv encourages all of us to do. And this is the missing link to move from good to great leadership. A very insightful and thoughtful collection of experiences and wisdom woven into the book. Will make us pause, reflect and reorient not just our leadership but our lives.'

—Mukul Deoras, President Asia-Pacific, Colgate-Palmolive Company

'Rajiv approaches the concept of leadership from a much deeper level than one would typically find. The questions he asks, the perspectives he brings and the framing he applies have benefited me enormously. An understanding of his approach will help any leader increase their effectiveness and create a future with clarity.'

—Sri Rajan, Former Chairman, Bain and Company India

'The journey of personal mastery described in this book is close to my heart. As you grow in your leadership, you will certainly appreciate the significance of this path and the simple but profound underlying insights lucidly captured by Rajiv.'

—Rajesh Jejurikar, Executive Director, Auto and Farm Sectors, Mahindra & Mahindra

'This profound and inspiring book is a must-read for leaders and aspiring leaders who wish to be authentic and impactful. Rajiv lucidly illustrates the centrality of 'self-mastery' in one's leadership journey, synthesized from thousands of hours spent coaching leaders in critical roles. As a direct beneficiary of his coaching, I am delighted that he is making his thoughts and methods available to a larger audience in this book.'

—**Raman Ramachandran Ph.D. Former Chairman & MD, BASF India Ltd; MD & CEO, PI Industries**

'Topical and much needed perspective on a range of issues at the core of leadership. Avoiding the normal, standard approaches, Rajiv shows us how to grow leadership by strengthening our inner self. Impactfully. Captures well the essence of the work he has been doing in transforming lives and leadership approaches.'

—**Ashok Ramchandran, Group Executive President—Group Human Resources, Aditya Birla Group**

'When a coaching conversation moves smoothly but is highly impactful, you know you have found a top-class coach. From starting the coaching programme to inspiring leaders at TCS, Rajiv has that kind of effortless impact on all and it reflects in his book. *Inside-Out Leadership* is full of learnings, simply put, yet deeply impactful. It forces you to examine yourself and offers great practical tips for current and potential leaders.'

—**Dr. Ritu Anand, Chief Leadership and Diversity Officer, Tata Consultancy Services**

'This book is an amazing culmination of Rajiv's insights and learnings. It is liberating leaders by highlighting that the secret to enhancing their effectiveness is within their control thereby empowering them to take control of their life and their destiny. The short exercises are a great way to reinforce applications of these learnings.'

—**Dr. Raju Mistry, President and Global Chief People Officer, Cipla**

'Rajiv Vij's message in *Inside-Out Leadership* inspires personal mastery and authentic leadership for leaders at all levels. He provides the reader with a blueprint to examine personal values, inner beliefs, and what's required for self-mastery. Revealing insights and wonderfully written, this is a timely book, and a must read for anyone charged with leading and making a difference.'

—**Brendan Kelly, Former Global Head of Leadership and Talent, Credit Suisse Group**

'Great leaders become so because of their focus on inner transformation. Drawn from his enormous executive coaching experience, the key insights articulated by Rajiv can help any leader embark on such a transformation. I found these insights comprehensive and extremely helpful in enabling us to calibrate ourselves and work on becoming a better leader.'

—**Krish Shankar, Executive Vice President, Group Head—Human Resource Development, Infosys**

INSIDE-OUT LEADERSHIP

16 radical insights
successful leaders wish
they had discovered sooner

Rajiv Vij

PENGUIN

VIKING

An imprint of Penguin Random House

VIKING

USA | Canada | UK | Ireland | Australia
New Zealand | India | South Africa | China | Singapore

Viking is part of the Penguin Random House group of companies
whose addresses can be found at global.penguinrandomhouse.com

Published by Penguin Random House India Pvt. Ltd
4th Floor, Capital Tower 1, MG Road,
Gurugram 122 002, Haryana, India

Penguin
Random House
India

First published by Westland Business, an imprint of Westland Publications Private Limited, in 2021
This edition published in Viking by Penguin Random House India in 2023

ISBN 9780670098064

Typeset by R. Ajith Kumar
Printed at Replika Press Pvt. Ltd, India

To my late parents

Contents

Applying the *Inside-Out* Approach: Mind

Applying the *Inside-Out* Approach: Soul

Applying the *Inside-Out* Approach: Wisdom and Balance

Foreword

I WAS RAISED IN A BUSINESS FAMILY, AND HENCE THERE WAS A NATURAL expectation by society that I would pursue an education preparing me for a career in industry. Yet, the idea of my life's path being preordained didn't sit well with me. In particular, I abhorred the thought of being privileged to run the family business without having earned the right to do so. I was determined to chart my own path and pursue my own passions.

Thus, I decided not to ignore my strong and intuitive interest in the creative fields of art, design, film and photography. However, being a little wary of departing too far from the sciences, in which I had excelled at school, I chose to explore architecture, since it seemed to combine an ideal blend of both left- and right-brained traits.

I applied for, and received admission to the J.J. College of Architecture in Mumbai. For a while, everything seemed to go according to plan. But then, destiny revealed its hand. Soon after I started college, we went on strike to press for university accreditation. I found myself joining protest marches at the Fort area in Mumbai. After nine months of seemingly never-ending protests, I began to feel like I was wasting precious time; I decided it was time for me to leave. It was then that I applied to Harvard University to study film, which was my other passion, after receiving a scholarship to attend the college. A liberal arts education would allow me the freedom to explore diverse fields without constraint. I only needed to specialise when choosing a graduate school. I felt truly liberated.

However, it didn't take long for me to experience my first lesson in humility. Although I had been particularly good at English in school, my first university English-course grade turned out to be a C. All that well-earned pride was quickly punctured. The pressure of performing among the super-achievers in my class was getting to me. There were days I thought of quitting and going back home. Fortunately, I didn't give up. I decided to just dig in and to just work hard. And that was my second lesson—the enormous value of resilience.

A liberal arts curriculum is like a sandbox; it allows you to play with a wide number of subjects so that you can uncover what your true calling is. During my experiments with the myriad disciplines on offer, I can never forget Prof. Robert Nozick's seminar on the philosophy of Sri Aurobindo! It was ironic that I had travelled all the way to Cambridge, Massachusetts to study the teachings of an Indian philosopher but my learning from that course has stayed with me all these years and shaped the person I have become. Aurobindo's essays became my personal guide to building greater self-awareness. Till date, those teachings have significantly influenced my perception of who I am and why I am here.

At the end of all my experimentation, I graduated with honours—magna cum laude—majoring in cinema and photography and making a thesis film on the Kumbh Mela which was very well received. With that project, I felt complete. I realised that I had chosen the long-winding, rebellious but scenic route but eventually had succeeded in proving to myself that I could survive without the protection of my family's ecosystem. I was now willing to engage in business on my own terms.

In a nutshell, what I learnt through my school and college years is the profound importance of three human traits in life: self-awareness, humility and resilience.

For the past thirty years, I have had the privilege to lead a large organisation. We have had several successes. We have also encountered some failures. Staying equanimous through the ups and downs of life and business is not always easy. However, self-awareness, humility and resilience have been great personal allies on this journey.

I've found that self-awareness is critical for effective leadership. Unless you are clear about who you are and what you want your life to be about, you'll struggle to make sense of your life and work. When I assess or hire new leaders, I am always trying to gauge their level of self-awareness. How well do they understand themselves, how comfortable are they in their own skin, how clear are they about their strengths and weaknesses and how committed they are to pursue what's most important to them. Asking such probing questions matters.

So what defines leadership? It's the extent of your followership. To have followership, you need to be self-assured. You need to be acutely aware whether you are a strategist or an executor, a thinker or a doer, an ideas person or a pragmatic manager, a risk-taker or risk-averse. You can accordingly surround yourself with people who possess complementary skills. But when you are insecure or unsure of yourself, you find it challenging to be an inspiration for your colleagues and develop followership.

Followership also requires engaging your team members in collectively creating a vision and empowering them to achieve that vision. Good leaders own the vision and the ideas to achieve it. Great leaders help their team members own the vision and the pathway to achieve it.

That brings me to the second quality: humility.

Humility is the ability to have a modest view of one's self-importance. Unfortunately, the more successful you become, the higher the risk of this trait becoming a casualty. I find this trend starts early on. I notice that the extent of humility is usually inversely proportional to the prestige of the educational institution young managers come from. Some of them, from the most well-known colleges, find it hard to defer to other people's views in a team. Leaders with an unusually high sense of self-importance struggle to bring people along on the journey to greatness. They lose followership and are unable to create sustainable long-term results.

The third trait that I value is resilience. Just as death is an integral part of life, failure is a part of pursuing success. Every successful leader has had his fair share of failures. Setbacks in business and life are always going to be around the corner. Instead of worrying about a setback or letting it bring us down, how about actually embracing the setback? It's one of the questions I often get asked by many of the managers, younger ones in particular. How do we deal with failure? Here's a three-step process that has worked for me.

Step one is to recognise the negative emotions. With any setback, you are likely to feel sad, frustrated and fearful. Be self-aware to acknowledge these feelings. Sit with them. Feel the terror and the tears. Secondly, make peace with these feelings. Instead of suppressing these emotions or wishing for them to quickly go away, embrace them. As our scriptures suggest, instead of resisting this state, accept it. Absorb the feelings, experience them and be willing to live with them. Take time off, go for a swim, go away on the weekend or engage in your hobby. And finally, I have noticed that if you are a driven person, you will soon get bored of self-pity and will be keen to get into the swing of things. You will inevitably want to start exploring how to move on and what to do next...

The *Inside-Out* approach to leadership, described in this book, is close to my heart. It speaks not only to the three qualities of effective leadership that I just described, but also to many more. It provides a complete framework to evolve from being a good leader to becoming a great one. The book in your hands is a seminal work that has the power to significantly influence your life and leadership. There's nothing closer to the truth than the perspective that you need to consciously and consistently work on your inner self to bring out your best external self to the world. I know the ideas in the book are not mere theories but rooted in practices that leaders have benefitted from in a big way.

I trust you make the most of this book, and use it as a personal guide to help you navigate your own journey to becoming a great leader, Inside-Out.

Anand G. Mahindra

Introduction

EVERY GOOD LEADER CAN BE A GREAT ONE.

I have been coaching leaders for over a decade and a half now. I have worked with leaders from a wide range of backgrounds—country managers of the largest multinationals and entrepreneurs of small and medium enterprises; those from the private sector and the not-for-profit sector; Asians, Americans, Europeans; from a twenty-seven year old to a seventy-seven year old. These leaders have been based in over fifteen countries, including Australia, Japan, China, Singapore, India, the US and the UK. About a third of them have been women.

They have worked with me on diverse areas, ranging from enhancing their leadership effectiveness, making an impact, creating inspirational teams and finding their true calling to reducing stress, improving work–life balance, deepening relationships and experiencing greater happiness.

Among all these engagements, two things stand out. The first is that everyone has a greater self, and that everyone has the potential to discover it. Everyone has the choice to learn, change and grow to be a better leader and every good leader can become *great*!

The other thing that shines through from these engagements—and it is not only of paramount importance but also often gets ignored—is that the journey to greater leadership effectiveness is rooted in enhancing one's personal effectiveness. What work leaders do to reform their inner selves is essential to experiencing outward success. The journey of inner transformation supports leaders not only in moving from 'good' to 'great', but also in creating a happier and more fulfilling life.

That's what *Inside-Out Leadership* is all about—focusing within to effect change in outer experiences and external outcomes; investing in personal growth as a conduit to professional growth; undertaking the journey of personal mastery as a pathway to achieving leadership mastery.

Through this book, I hope to share with you some key lessons related to this unique philosophy. These are things I have learnt over my coaching journeys with various leaders: the common blind spots that leaders develop over time, the alternative ways of being and leading and the pathway for moving from good to great.

I have chosen to distil the essence of my learnings into sixteen powerful insights. My clients have benefitted considerably from these, and I hope you will too. As the journey of growing your leadership effectiveness entails embracing certain fundamental shifts, not just in behaviour but also in your thoughts, attitudes and approaches, I describe each of these insights as a significant shift from one state of leadership to another. You will find chapters that discuss moving the focus of leadership from primarily delivering results to making a lasting impact; moving from a directive and task-oriented leadership style to a more coach-like manner that inspires the team to be the best they can be; moving from operating from a place of self-doubt and insecurity to leading with inner strength and confidence; moving from carrying on with limiting beliefs to cultivating the right mindset; and moving from chasing short-term life and career goals to living and leading with purpose.

Before we jump into the discussion on leadership transformation, however, it may be worth addressing a few basic questions:

What is leadership?

Who can be considered a leader?

How do you acquire leadership skills?

To my mind, the environmental activist who mobilises a mass digital campaign to influence government policy is a leader, as is the teacher who skilfully helps numerous children discover and shape their vision of the future. The public servant who, passionately driven by a social cause, like moderating income inequality, positively impacts the lives of citizens; the first girl from her village to attend college, who then inspires many others to follow suit; the businessman who creates a nurturing environment for his team to create an innovative technology app; the research scientist who spends hours in the lab mastering her domain and influences the direction of future work in her field; the parent who encourages her children to be curious, to learn and explore more of their interests and to be the best they can be—each one of these people is a leader.

Here's the thing . . . most people confuse leadership with titles. It's easy to associate only certain hierarchical positions in certain arenas—businesses, corporations or governmental institutions—with 'real leadership'. I'm not denying that top management roles can provide a larger canvas to make greater impact. That said, examples of great leadership can be spotted in our everyday life too. All you have to do is look around you.

The point? Leadership is a *verb*. It is defined by the actions of an individual, and not necessarily limited by the scope or description of someone's job.

There are many ways to define leadership. The one I like, and has stuck with me, is both simple and instructive: '*Leadership is the art of inspiring others to deliberately create an outcome that wouldn't have otherwise been accomplished.*' To simplify this further, leadership is made up of three key ingredients—the idea of a desired outcome, the notion of inspiring others and the underlying value added by the leader, without which the specific result may not have been achieved.

Great leaders are able to engage others in creating a *collective vision*—a lofty goal that the people involved would not have considered possible otherwise—and inspiring and supporting them towards actualising the vision. Most importantly, they do so in a way that is both responsible and sustainable. They are mindful of the long-term impact of their actions and vision, not only on their immediate area of work but also on the wider society.

An important next question is how do you acquire leadership skills? Some people are simply born with strong leadership traits. They are naturally driven to take initiative on ideas they believe in from an early age. Some examples I've come across are a passionate high school student who successfully persuaded the school management to improve working conditions for the cleaning staff for the sake of the staff's dignity, and an eighteen year old who campaigned for raising awareness about gay and lesbian communities among school students.

Others acquire these skills through life experiences. Think of examples and instances from your own life that have contributed to building your leadership capacity. Right from your school days, various activities and roles, such as participating in or leading a sports team, a music band or community initiatives, shape your understanding of teamwork, conflict resolution, effective communication and leadership. As you enter the workforce, you have many more opportunities to take on leadership roles, even at the junior-most levels. Participating in your division's initiatives, contributing to the generation of new business ideas or raising your hand to get involved in cross-functional groups like a women's network or a health and wellness club, build on these skills. As you rise in the organisation, roles that allow you to lead teams or make a higher impact on your organisation naturally lead to a growing understanding of leadership.

You may also acquire some of these skills through osmosis—by observing other leaders in action. These could be your parents, teachers, seniors at work or any role models in the community that you look up to. If you are lucky enough to have a mentor in your professional or personal life, you may learn and benefit from their guidance. In addition, structured learning opportunities such as studying leadership at an MBA school or attending leadership development programmes at work help enhance these skills. Feedback from colleagues and family members may also help you refine your skills.

What holds average leaders back from breaking through?

In my experience, there are three reasons individuals reach a plateau in their learning and growth as leaders much sooner than they should.

Firstly, many a time, there is a paucity of suitable role models in their life. Speaking broadly, I hope you'll agree that leadership has failed us in recent times. Global political leadership has been marred by corruption, lobbying by political donors and business interests, short-term orientation towards winning elections and leaders' inability to inspire society towards action on the gravest global issues of our time, like climate change. The trust in business leadership has weakened as employees and their families continue to witness various corporate scandals across different industries. Even the social sector has not been immune to this. Besides, the yawning gap in rewards between the senior-most leaders and everyone else has contributed to widespread disillusionment.

But then, the quality of leadership is nothing but a reflection of the state of our society, isn't it? That brings me to the second reason leaders do not end up fulfilling their personal potential.

As a society, and especially in our capacity as leaders, we are progressively disconnected with our inner selves. While economic growth offers tremendous choice in every aspect of our life, right from education and careers to recreation and travel, we seem to be out of sync with those core personal values that enable one to make such choices. We fail to be clear on a higher personal purpose that guides our professional pursuits. And with a disproportionately high focus on short-term shareholder returns, there's been a significant dilution and, in some cases, a complete absence, of clarity of the purpose for which an organisation exists in the first place. In the process, leaders often fall prey to the temptations of choosing convenience over righteousness and personal gratification over longer-term organisational interests.

Driven by a fast-paced corporate life, most leaders do not create time for structured reflection. As a result, they fail to look within and deepen their level of self-awareness. Hence, the unhealthy practices that usually get picked up when doing any activity for a long time, like the mistakes that creep up in a golf swing or a tennis serve, do not get noticed or addressed. We become too comfortable operating on autopilot.

When you are succeeding, it's easy to not question how you could improve what you do and slip into limiting patterns of old habits. Over time, some of these habits become blind spots. The approaches that supported you in getting to senior positions are not always the ones required to be effective in those roles. Not learning to step back and objectively observe your own thoughts, beliefs, mindsets and behaviours can hold you back from refreshing and upgrading your leadership style. You can simply become stuck in your approach.

Finally, what can often add to the challenges of your pursuit of excellence as a leader is the lack of practical resources to support you in making the changes you wish to make. Even if you receive relevant feedback or pay attention to limiting personal traits, you may struggle to find practical solutions. Annual appraisals bring out what you need to improve on, but do not always have a follow-through on how to actually go about making the desired changes and put them into action. So, although you become aware that you need to be bolder in your decisions or not be aggressive with your colleagues, you may be unsure of *how* to be so, particularly if these are deep-seated personality traits for you. What approaches do you need to employ to make this change possible?

Inside-Out Leadership aims to fill these gaps. The pages within will make you pause and reflect, and assist you in deepening your self-awareness and discovering your greater self. This book will provide you with tools and practical ideas to support you in your ongoing journey of leadership growth. Yes, some individuals are born with the skills for leadership, but I believe that with conscious effort most of us can grow into it.

The pathway of moving from good to great leadership elaborated in this book directly responds to the challenges of leading in modern times, whether in business, public service or the social sector. Whether you are an experienced leader or have just begun your leadership journey, I hope some of the sixteen Insights described in the following pages address your unique and personal leadership challenges. I trust that the underlying approach of facilitating mindset shifts will empower you to deal with any current or future leadership challenges in an effective way. The opportunity to embark on a journey towards personal mastery that is offered here will not only help you connect, and work, with your inner self, but also support you in leading from a place of character, vision, purpose and inspiration. In my experience, pursuing this powerful journey will allow you to create lasting, sustainable and positive impact. It will also help you discover greater balance, happiness and meaning in your life.

Prior to discovering my calling and starting my coaching practice, I had a successful career that included significant leadership roles in India and other parts of Asia. Although I reckon my ex-colleagues would describe me as highly successful, I am now more aware of the limitations of my leadership style. More importantly, I can relate to the challenges of my own inner experience—the sense of insecurity and self-doubt, my discomfort with confrontational situations or the less than optimal level of emotional resilience. Personally, if I had discovered the Insights captured in this book then, I'd have certainly done things differently in my leadership. My coaching practice has made me even more convinced that numerous other successful leaders out there feel the same need.

Before we dive into the sixteen Insights of great leadership, I do want to emphasise that the *Inside-Out* approach is the cornerstone of long-term and sustainable leadership effectiveness. The journey of superior leadership is as much about leading yourself as it is about leading others. Only when we work on our inner self, our emotional triggers and conditioned beliefs, only when we gain clarity on our life's purpose and only when we take responsibility for our thoughts and actions, do we transform as individuals and as leaders. I trust the Insights contained in this book, in the form of these key shifts, will alter not only your leadership style and how you are perceived by others around you, but most importantly, how you experience your own inner journey of work and life. I hope this book inspires you to become the person and the leader you are capable of becoming.

Finally, a word on how you can read and use this book. You may find that the book opens a can of worms when it comes to key challenges that leaders face in their day-to-day activities.

The first chapter is designed for you to identify some of your personal opportunities for leadership development. Following that, I introduce the *Inside-Out* approach for leadership transformation. The book is then divided into five sections where we get to apply this approach as a response to key leadership challenges. The five sections loosely correspond to the distinct opportunities a leader has for inner transformation in relation to their *impact* (enhancing strategy and effectiveness), *heart* (managing emotions, deepening relationships and inspiring others), *mind* (building the right mental attitude, managing stress, learning to let go and overcoming limiting and conditioned beliefs), *soul* (connecting with a higher purpose, discovering their calling and cultivating mindfulness) and *wisdom and balance* (creating balance and sustaining the journey of change). I have attempted to keep each of the Insights as individual chapters and as stand-alone as possible. Hence, if you feel drawn to reading certain themes or Insights more than others, please feel free to do so. However, I would strongly recommend that you familiarise yourself with the *Inside-Out* approach first because it is foundational to the journey of change. You will find some short exercises at the end of each Insight that are aimed at supporting your personal reflections and your own journey of discovering and fulfilling your true potential.

With that out of the way, let's get started!

Key Leadership Challenges

Challenges are what make life interesting;
overcoming them is what makes life meaningful.

— JOSHUA J. MARINE, American author

BEFORE WE START THE DISCUSSION ON THE TRANSFORMATIVE SHIFTS THAT separate great leaders from their average counterparts, it is important to highlight the key challenges leaders usually experience.

Leaders possess unique and special talents, but let's face it . . . they are human too. Like everyone else, they have their share of failings. Like everyone else, they have their blind spots. Yet, here's something I've experienced over and over in my coaching practice—success often makes it harder to distance yourself from your achievements to assess yourself objectively. As a refreshing contrast, the most successful leaders consciously seek feedback. They are always in the search for new ways of leading and of being.

An awareness of the challenges you need to overcome as a leader can come through diverse channels. Difficulties in some areas of your professional or personal life might help you recognise certain patterns in your leadership style. For example, an inability to make an impact or inspire colleagues, a tendency to feel overwhelmed, or experiencing high levels of stress may trigger you to pay attention to these recurring challenges. You may also receive feedback from your stakeholders, your advisors, team members or business partners that prompts greater understanding. This could be formal and structured, as in the annual review, or informal in nature.

Moreover, you will likely get feedback (usually unsolicited!) in your personal life, from your family members or friends. Since we tend to be less guarded in our personal lives and find it easier to trust our family and friends, we just may be more open to constructive feedback in such an environment. This can help develop greater self-awareness. For example, if you frequently experience friction with your spouse or teenage children, it may prompt you to question your emotional temperament; this, in turn, may help you recognise how your emotional make-up might be affecting your relationships at work.

Over the past more than fifteen years, I have engaged with leaders on a wide variety of professional and personal challenges. However, here is a brief description of some of the key challenges that tend to surface the most frequently. You may notice some overlaps across the list, but each challenge presents a distinct hurdle.

Making an impact

For many leaders, taking their game to a higher level presents a significant challenge. If you experience this, you are quite likely already meeting your agreed goals, but you continue to get the feedback that you are not making enough impact. I get it—if you are hitting your numbers or other agreed goals, this can be frustrating to hear. Also, while most of the key performance indicators are usually easy to measure, an assessment of 'impact' can appear rather ambiguous or qualitative.

At leadership positions, you are evaluated on two dimensions, that of the two 'P's. The first 'P' refers to your *Performance* on agreed goals, while the second 'P' refers to the broader range of your leadership skills, and is hence considered indicative of your *Potential*. Often times, the perceived shortfall in your quality of impact is directly related to insufficient demonstration of leadership skills or the second 'P'. This might be a reflection of how strategic you are, how well you inspire your team, or how well you display corporate values. We'll explore this in greater detail later.

Being strategic

Some leaders naturally gravitate to having a strategic and long-term orientation towards their organisational goals. Others tend to thrive in driving operational excellence and successful execution of ideas. Great leaders are able to strike a healthy balance and are able to do both at appropriate points in time. They possess the capacity for bifocal vision: the ability to have both a long-term strategy and an appreciation that the strategy is only as good as its execution.

Personally, I find many more leaders are aspiring to become more strategic. Perhaps having done more operationally heavy roles in the past, they already possess the skills for execution excellence and are now ready to fill the gap in their strategic orientation. This skill is also integral to the ability to make an impact.

Readiness for whatever is the next big role for you

If you are one of the top-end performers and have demonstrated your potential for bigger roles, this maybe an area you identify with. Leaders in this space have generally received clear feedback that they are being considered for bigger roles and that they need to develop certain leadership traits to get past the last hurdle. This is where you can identify a great leader with a strong hold on their emotional quotient; some find it hard to acknowledge such feedback and accept that there is more room for development. Even those who do, however, may not necessarily be clear about *how* to go about building those traits or overcoming any limiting barriers.

Creating an inspired team

A common theme across leaders at all levels, this is typically articulated on the lines of, 'I have six direct reports and two of them are fantastic in taking initiative and delivering results, two of them are pretty good, and two are quite average. As a leadership team, while we are doing quite well and are consistently hitting our numbers, I don't think we are pulling our entire weight together. I think we have a lot of untapped potential. I have tried different things but would like to explore what else I could do to better tap into that potential.'

Further, depending on the leader's role, this challenge may also relate to motivating their larger team or organisation.

Interpersonal conflicts

When there are two or more people working together, there's always a risk of interpersonal friction. Organisations, by their very nature, are made up of a number of people. While the overarching goals of an organisation bring teams together, individuals vary in their personal motivations, beliefs and approaches. Individuals are also guided by their own ego and agendas. (No wonder interpersonal conflicts appear routinely in organisations!) Leaders may not only experience interpersonal conflicts directly with colleagues, they are also likely to be pulled into resolving such conflicts among their team members and peers. Such conflicts can be significantly detrimental to the morale of the team as well as to the achievement of organisational goals.

Lack of trust with key stakeholders

In many situations, while there may not be any noticeable interpersonal conflict, there's a lack of trust between the leader and some of his or her stakeholders. Trust is central to leadership effectiveness. If there's any trust deficit, the relationships are unlikely to be open and authentic. Lack of trust makes people shaky and unsteady in their decisions as well as interactions. They hold back their true thoughts and feelings. This then leads to a focus on self-preservation and self-interest and an inclination to align based on internal politics rather than what's best for the team or the organisation.

Unhealthy work-life balance

In the 24/7 work culture of most modern organisations, employees in general and leaders in particular are universally working long hours. I have witnessed this equally with leaders across businesses, industries and sectors. Sixty hours a week seems par for the course, with some leaders working close to eighty a week. Time management is a real struggle. This has only become more challenging in the new work-from-home environment where there are no boundaries between work and home. This has a wide-ranging impact on their professional and personal life. It reduces their ability to be mentally present in the moment and affects their temperament and judgment. Their productivity takes a beating, their health suffers and their personal relationships deteriorate.

With long hours and perpetual mental preoccupation being common challenges for today's leadership, finding a healthy balance is a perennial battle for most.

High levels of stress

With stress levels so high in the workplace, leaders are the ones to feel the heat directly. They experience the stress that is part and parcel of operating in a high-pressure work environment—from constantly working with ambitious goals, managing conflicts between short-term objectives and long-term vision, juggling stiff deadlines, dealing with crisis situations as well as facing high competition, difficult colleagues and demanding stakeholders. Leaders also feel the stress from the physical demands on their time, reflected in long hours, extensive travel and not enough rest for the body.

Moreover, some of us are more stress-prone than others. Any number of factors, such as one's emotional make-up, a tendency to seek perfection in everything, inability to inspire others, controlling nature, propensity to brood over setbacks, can contribute to the extent of stress one experiences. Leaders with a lower threshold for stress suffer first. They experience a lower sense of well-being, feel unfulfilled and desperately yearn for more peace of mind.

Aggressive personality

A certain level of aggression is revered in organisations. Aggression is associated with being determined and pushing towards your goals. It's almost as if showing aggression is symbolic of being tough enough to handle challenging situations. However, there's a thin line between thoughtful aggression and overaggression. Leaders with highly aggressive personalities usually struggle with creating a deep and trusting bond with their colleagues. They may also operate from a belief that fear is a powerful motivator for their team members. An aggressive approach usually makes leaders impatient, ineffective listeners and temperamental.

Here's something to note: leaders with these traits are not necessarily happy being this way. Many a time, they just can't help it. Faced with both, external resistance from colleagues and internal remorse, they are keen to reform this. They don't know if there's a more effective way to lead.

Soft-spoken and withdrawn

Then, there are leaders who fall on the other end of the spectrum to being aggressive. They have a predisposition for being permissive. They can be great at listening well, building consensus and being more deliberate with their decisions. They are generally well liked. However, they are inclined to avoid confrontation, give in easily, are uncomfortable saying no and tend to be quieter. This directly impacts their effectiveness. They hesitate to express their inner thoughts and feelings freely and hence risk not being adept at influencing others. They may also be limited in their ability to hold their team accountable. Unable to engage freely and authentically with their colleagues, they sometimes feel like a victim of their environment.

Excessive task-orientation

In my coaching, I have come across leaders who are highly task-oriented. They are too focused on achieving goals, sometimes without paying sufficient attention to their people. They have been told that they lack empathy, are not adept at understanding or responding to others' emotions and have a lower Emotional Quotient (EQ). Many leaders with a high Intelligence Quotient (IQ) and a drive for results become highly successful. Yet, at some point in their journey, they hit a roadblock. Lack of people-orientation becomes a serious limitation to their ability to inspire teams and deliver sustainable results. They usually bring their excessive task-orientation to their family life as well—a trait that is invariably unbearable for the rest of the family.

Managing global diversity

While this is a challenge for leaders in any cross-cultural environment, it seems to come up a fair bit among some of the Asian and Indian multinationals. As these organisations expand globally, organically or through acquisitions, their leaders are faced with a unique challenge. Used to a more hierarchical structure and leading a fairly homogenous team back home, managing a team with diverse cultural backgrounds and work ethos is a new test for them. In many geographies, leaders feel frustrated with their new team's slower response speed and lack of conformity to authority. Their teams, on the other hand—as much as they usually admire the leader's analytical capacity, tend to complain about the leader's directive approach.

Influencing without authority

Real leadership is not dictated by one's seniority or position in the hierarchy. It is not automatically conferred when you hit a certain pay-scale. It also has little to do with attributes such as taking charge and domineering through a situation.

Real leadership is about influencing others towards your point of view, and thus maximising their efforts towards achieving a goal. For a CEO, this extends well beyond the leadership team within the organisation; it extends to board members, industry bodies, regulatory institutions and social networks. Many leaders, while excellent at driving results with their teams, feel challenged in this area externally. Besides, leaders in all capacities need to influence their peers, and sometimes seniors, over whom they have no direct authority. This need gets amplified in organisations with a matrix structure. Some of the leaders find the process emotionally draining while others feel frustrated believing that there's too much politics to navigate. Nevertheless, great leaders acknowledge this is a crucial skill for them to develop.

Executive presence

Closely linked with the above theme is the notion of executive presence. Your executive presence is the sum of your confidence, credibility, communication and appearance—how well you listen and engage with others, articulate your own ideas and how you show up. Executive presence has a direct impact on the quality of attention you receive from others and the extent of followership you generate among them. The greater your role and responsibility, the more desired a trait executive presence becomes.

Happiness and fulfilment

Like every other human being on the planet, leaders too are searching for happiness and fulfilment. As they reflect on their personal journey, some of them recognise that while driving themselves at breakneck speed gets their adrenaline pumping, it does not always contribute to sustained happiness. For many, achieving ambitious business goals is exciting, yet not deeply fulfilling. For some, it's their mental and emotional wiring which makes them prone to unhappiness, which gets accentuated in a stressful work environment. They are hungry for ideas to experience greater happiness, peace and balance in their life.

What next?

When I spend time with leaders, I find many of them also questioning their life direction. As an extension of the previous challenge, they feel jaded at work and in life. While they are not necessarily unhappy, they are wondering if there's an alternative path that would perhaps serve them better. Some could be feeling stagnant in their roles, some burnt out, and yet others could be searching for greater meaning in their work and in life. This need for creating a new life seems to come up a lot with leaders in their forties or fifties. This time of their life also seems to coincide with experiencing some form of midlife crisis—it's a time of varying professional and personal challenges and setbacks, when individuals feel the need for greater self-reflection. Moreover, some of the leaders may have reached a reasonable level of financial comfort and finally feel secure enough to entertain the idea of pursuing dreams they are deeply passionate about.

Some observations

As you read though this list, you may notice that many of these challenges are interrelated. Not being strong in one area impacts your level of strength in other areas too. Any one challenge can get manifested in multiple ways. Your headstrong and aggressive personality may influence your ability to create an inspired team, build trust with colleagues, make an impact, manage stress and experience deeper happiness. The flip side is that working through any one of these significant challenges positively influences your professional—and personal—effectiveness in a multidimensional way. In fact, in many situations, it's really a few of your limiting personality traits that are at the source of the variety of challenges you may experience at work. Reforming such traits can have far-reaching implications for you. We will look at that as the first Insight in the next chapter.

Given that these challenges and their solutions are interlinked, and to avoid repetition of ideas, I have tried to address them by examining their underlying source, their root cause. The sixteen key shifts, what I term Insights, articulated in the following chapters are in response to that. The first three Insights lay out a framework for the *Inside-Out* journey of change. The rest of the Insights have been divided into five categories, on the basis of their central theme. The Insights aim to give you the roadmap to a journey that will unleash both your leadership and your personal potential.

Personal actions

1. Reflecting on the above list, list your key personal leadership challenges.
2. Based on the feedback you have received from time to time at work or outside, list any other development opportunities.

The *Inside-Out* Approach

Insight 1

From Professional Battles
to Personal Mastery

It's not the mountain we conquer, but ourselves.

– EDMUND HILLARY, mountaineer and philanthropist

INSIDE-OUT LEADERSHIP IS FOUNDED ON THE PRINCIPLE OF DEEP PERSONAL development—the work you do to reform your inner self. It takes as central the premise that as you grow your self-awareness, cultivate healthy thoughts and beliefs, enhance emotional regulation and commit to serving a higher purpose, your leadership ability and leadership effectiveness automatically go up. The work you do within shines through in your external conduct as a leader.

To begin understanding this, we need to appreciate that in leadership positions, you cannot differentiate between professional effectiveness and personal effectiveness. Who you are at the core, as a person, begins to show quickly. Whether you lean more towards being controlling or empowering, perfectionist or disorganised, big picture or detail-oriented, pushy or passive gets reflected in your leadership. Not only does the word spread among your colleagues quickly but, in fact, your reputation precedes you in new roles as well. Now, this is relevant for people at all levels, in any organisation, not leaders alone. At leadership positions, though, you are in the spotlight, and everyone, from seniors and peers to team members, is watching you.

If you are committed to becoming a better leader than you currently are, it is pertinent that you pay attention to building yourself. As an executive coach, I always ask the sponsoring organisation to allow me to work with the leader as a person as a 'whole', so that we don't limit the coaching to the formal role they may hold. The leaders invariably find the work we do on goals linked to their personal growth and personality traits the most enriching. Often, it's the shifts people make on a personal level that have the greatest impact on their leadership.

Let me give you an example.

Anindya is the head of finance for a multinational bank in India. He is talented and is one of the high-performing executives in the bank. During our first coaching session, we discussed that among other goals, one of the areas Anindya was keen to work on was managing his stress better and being more at peace. Constant preoccupation with work was not allowing him to enjoy his work fully and also impacting his relationships outside of work, such as with his family. Besides, he had no time to focus on his personal health. While learning to be more at peace seems like a relatively personal goal, as you will see, working on it directly shaped his leadership abilities.

We talked about multiple approaches to manage his stress. However, for the sake of our discussion here, let me highlight two key ones. Firstly, Anindya decided that he had to start leaving office latest by 6.30 p.m., instead of the 8 p.m. that he had gotten used to. This forced him to explore ways to be more productive at work. He recognised the need to be more strategic in his approach and prioritise the most important tasks. He also realised that he needed to delegate in a much smarter manner.

At the same time, Anindya decided to refine some of the personality traits that he believed came in the way of his being a calmer and more relaxed person. Becoming less of a perfectionist and learning to let go of the need to control all outcomes were two prominent shifts that allowed him to be less preoccupied with work, start trusting more and become comfortable with delegating effectively.

As he got better at managing his time and his personality traits, he became more at peace, and improved the quality of the time he spent with his family. He also felt fitter, as he started going to the gym thrice a week. In the process, he became more productive at work, and built on his overall leadership effectiveness, creating an environment that empowered his team—changes that were very visible and were validated by his seniors.

Towards personal mastery

Inside-Out leadership takes the idea of raising personal effectiveness to a whole new level. Committing to this journey requires that you shift your focus from external events to your inner experiences; from simply gaining more business knowledge to also learning more about yourself; from blaming others for your performance to taking greater personal responsibility.

Edmund Hilary, along with Tenzing Norgay, was the first person to climb Mount Everest. As he returned to the base camp, amidst all the celebrations, he was interviewed by journalists. The reporters were keen to know how he managed to accomplish what no one had ever been able to. One of them asked him with great curiosity, *'What does it feel like to conquer the tallest mountain in the world?'* Edmund Hilary reflected on this for a bit and then responded, *'It's not the mountain we conquer, but ourselves.'*

That, to my mind, is the essence of the idea of the *Inside-Out* approach. It is to recognise that what's holding you back from becoming a greater leader is your own self—specifically, your inability to examine yourself in an objective way and make necessary amends. Blinded partly by your past success and partly by your failure to create time to pause and reflect, you may overlook your limiting beliefs, personal biases, dysfunctional behaviours or even your relationship with your work, which delays your growth as a person and, in turn, as a leader.

Inside-Out leadership is not about 'mastering' professional skills alone, but about becoming deeply aware of who you are, about the direction you want your life to steer in and about relating to a higher purpose in your professional pursuits. *It is not about winning the battles of business or winning the next big deal (normally the greatest preoccupation of business leaders), but about winning the battles of your mind.* It is about reforming our traits of greed, envy, anger, insecurity and judgment, and replacing them with authenticity, wholesomeness, generosity, resilience and compassion. The *Inside-Out* approach is not about reaching a specific business or personal goal, but about a path of personal growth that we *choose* to embark on. It's about raising your level of self-awareness, living in alignment with your values, clarifying your life's purpose and taking responsibility for your thoughts and actions. In that way, it is about working towards gaining personal mastery.

This inner work shines through not only in good times, but even more so in times of crisis. During the recent pandemic, some leaders showed tremendous vision, character, resilience and compassion while others reacted passively to the turn of events. If you take a moment to reflect on leaders you thought were the most effective during that time, hopefully, you can notice signs of their higher self-awareness, sense of purpose and self-responsibility—their progress with personal mastery.

I have researched this area for over a decade now, and based on both my personal journey and my coaching experience, I believe travelling down this path has wide-ranging ramifications. I would argue that right from positively impacting your professional choices, leadership effectiveness and quality of relationships, this journey could go on to shape your state of happiness, your contribution to society and your level of fulfilment.

Leadership quotients

To clarify the concept further, let me expand on the idea of personal mastery by placing it in the context of other prevalent leadership concepts. Management literature is filled with tools to assess an individual's leadership potential. For the longest time, an individual's IQ was thought to be one of the key indicators of leadership potential. Considered to represent the person's ability to think sharply, it suggested that the smartest person in the room should be the leader. This notion assumed that the smartest person would be the best equipped to come up with the most effective leadership strategy.

In the 1980s, along came the idea of EQ, the Emotional Quotient. Popularised by thought leaders with a background in psychology, EQ measures an individual's ability to understand, empathise and negotiate with other people. Daniel Goleman, an internationally renowned psychologist, in particular, was instrumental in questioning the notion of IQ as the sole determinant of one's leadership potential.

Today, EQ is an important yardstick to assess leadership potential. It is easy to appreciate why. To attain success, you not only need to possess solid cognitive skills to develop the right strategies, but also the ability to galvanise the rest of the organisation towards effectively coming around and executing that strategy. EQ is a key differentiator among leaders with comparable IQs, because it facilitates their capacity to connect with others and motivate them. I am sure that from your experiences, too, you will be able to identify leaders who are successful primarily because of their higher emotional intelligence.

Then, there is the idea of the Spiritual Quotient, SQ—a relatively nascent idea but the one I am most fascinated by. Not to be confused with any religious (or related) connotations, SQ essentially reflects the extent of a leader's self-realisation. It captures the leader's level of self-awareness and their sense of self-responsibility. This is a measure of what they deeply stand for, their non-negotiable values, their strength of character and their commitment to a clear personal purpose and how it maps out to the organisation's mission. It emphasises not *what* they do, but *why* do they choose to do it. It also reflects their sense of responsibility and appreciation of the impact of their actions on the world around them.

I believe SQ is the final bastion of leadership growth. When leaders grow their SQ, they operate from a healthy combination of self-confidence and humility, passion and letting go and producing results and creating sustainable contribution. They are guided by a strong desire to serve others, not merely to grow their institution. The reason I am bringing this into our conversation is because, to my mind, acquiring a higher SQ is no different from progressing on the journey of personal mastery. While you need raw intelligence and the ability to connect, inspire and influence people, operating from a place of higher self-awareness, conscience and purpose helps you break through to new levels of leadership effectiveness.

Here's another way to look at the idea of personal mastery. Junior management roles are about *managing tasks*—specific and well-defined activities, like carrying on certain factory operations or responding to customer queries. Middle-level management is about *managing processes*. A manager in such a role is focused on improving the efficiency of processes, comprising several tasks. The process could be related to writing software code for an application or the steps a new visitor to a hotel has to go through from arrival at the taxi drop-off point to getting to their room and getting their bags. Senior management and leadership roles, besides developing suitable strategy, are about *managing people*. Most leaders say that they spend nearly as much as 50 per cent of their time on people issues, whether to do with their immediate team members or the wider employee base. Their key concerns are related to creating a suitable organisational culture, aligning teams to the broader organisational vision, instituting systems to attract, retain and grow talent and so forth.

Here's the insightful distinction. The most effective leaders are the ones who know how to *manage themselves*. They manage their time, priorities, temper, insecurities, ego, passion, mental chatter and relationships better than most others. While much harder to achieve, this is the key to mastering leadership. Leaders who pay attention to this aspect become such role models that everyone around them wants to follow them. They no longer need to put in a huge effort towards leading others. Mahatma Gandhi did not have an organisational title or even a clearly defined role. However, it was his way of life, governed by strong morals, a selfless desire to serve and an insatiable search for the truth, that dictated his unparalleled followership.

Research evidence

While we will get to discuss more about the different aspects of this self-work in the following Insights, I would like to highlight the strong evidence in favour of personal mastery as the key to outstanding leadership. As part of my research, I have, over time, interviewed a number of industry leaders in India and others based in Singapore and the US. These include leaders like Anand Mahindra, Harsh Mariwala, Keki Dadiseth, K.V. Kamath, Nandan Nilekani, Narayana Murthy, S. Ramadorai and Uday Kotak. I was curious to learn their thoughts about the connection, if any, between the idea of personal mastery and leadership. Specifically, I asked them questions such as:

* Is the notion of personal mastery relevant to leadership, and if so, how?
* How does personal mastery manifest itself for you in your workplace?
* How do you acquire it?

Here's what I learnt from them. While each one of them had a slightly different description of the concept of personal mastery, they all concurred that progress on the journey of personal mastery is a true differentiator between good leaders and outstanding ones. They felt leaders with greater self-awareness, a strong value system and a clear sense of personal purpose tend to make more effective long-term leaders. Some went on to say that while identifying their own successors, the extent of personal mastery of the candidates has been one of the key criteria, although often not explicitly stated, for their evaluation.

In terms of how mastery over the self manifests in a leaders' operating style, they shared that it's visible in a leader in multiple ways— in a leader's strong sense of character, greater grit, determination and resilience, confidence in developing successors, better work-life balance as well as higher sensitivity towards the social impact of their actions on the broader community. A few leaders did point out that the mere manifestation of any of these aspects, like greater work-life balance or involvement in social issues, may not necessarily and automatically indicate greater personal mastery.

Lastly, I asked them for guidance, based on their personal experience, on how leaders could acquire these traits. The answers essentially pointed to some kind of a role model in their own life who had deeply influenced their outlook towards work and life. Someone had a nurturing grandparent who positively shaped their values; someone else recalled an inspirational teacher who made a big impact on their life. Many leaders benefitted from having a mentor at work. A couple of leaders also expressed the influence of exposure to philosophical thought and spiritual teachings.

Besides, many of them highlighted the role personal or professional crisis can play in altering a leader's perspective and behaviour. The crisis could be the loss of a job or being passed over for an important promotion; it could be a personal health situation or a troubled marriage; it could be an institutional crisis involving clients, investors, donors, the board or employees. Such situations make us reflect—*what's most important to us and why; what's the meaning of life and what is our role in it; how can we live a life aligned to our deeper values?* If we can harness the energy of such inner turmoil, it enables us to live and lead from a very different place. It adds the qualities of mindfulness, character and humility to our sense of passion and progress—a powerful mix that boosts our own personal mastery. All the same, most of the leaders highlighted that personal mastery is a lifelong journey and requires conscious, ongoing effort.

Nevertheless, I am sure you have come across leaders who are successful but far removed from any notion of personal mastery. In fact, some even have a strong disregard for such ideas when it comes to management and leadership. They believe that the only thing that matters is the results. To them, the means are secondary and the idea of working on the self rather woolly. This approach has some serious drawbacks.

Firstly, their leadership is unlikely to produce *sustainable* quality results in the long term. The limitations of their approach are bound to catch up with them. They may stagnate, experience burnout or just lose followership. Secondly, such an approach is unlikely to serve society well. A single-minded, stubborn focus on results invariably conflicts with the interests of employees, clients and the broader community. Moreover, no matter how successful such leaders become, without paying adequate attention to personal growth, they may struggle to experience deeper happiness and meaning in their progress.

Personal mastery is the cornerstone of the journey of *Inside-Out* transformation. The following two chapters build on this approach, and in the subsequent chapters, you will see the application of this approach to the various leadership challenges we talked about earlier.

Personal actions

1. List any leaders you may have come across who are well advanced on the path of personal mastery. What do you notice as their key traits?

How is their progress on this journey reflected in their thinking or actions?

2. How do you assess your IQ, EQ and SQ? Can you spot gaps and identify room for development?

Insight 2

From Changing Others to Changing Self

The real voyage of discovery consists not in seeking new lands but seeing with new eyes.

– MARCEL PROUST, French philosopher

AS YOU COMMIT TO THIS JOURNEY OF PERSONAL MASTERY, ONE OF THE foremost lessons you'll learn is that change has to happen within you. We often tend to externalise our challenges. When we face a roadblock in any professional or personal situation, we are quick to blame our circumstances or the other people involved in the situation.

Do the following statements from work or personal life sound familiar?

- *My boss is too intimidating.*
- *This peer of mine is just not trustworthy.*
- *Everyone here works late; there's no way I can leave early!*
- *Some of the individuals in my team just don't have the hunger to achieve.*
- *We have been married for twenty years, and my spouse doesn't really care for my feelings any longer.*
- *Our kids don't listen to us anymore!*

What strikes you as the common theme among these statements?

They share the subconscious belief that the source of the person's ineffectiveness or unhappiness is someone else. That whatever is coming in the way of their progress is *outside* of them. That if only other people could change, their life would improve dramatically. That they are helpless within the current circumstances.

We often tend to think in this manner, but the truth is that much of the change is within you. The good news is that when you change within, irrespective of the people and the circumstances around you, you start to experience a different reality. Now, let me be clear. I'm not asking you to shift blame to yourself, but to alter your thoughts, perceptions and behaviour patterns so you can engage with the same circumstances differently.

Blaming others, wishing, waiting and hoping for external circumstances or other people to change creates a very different reality from the one you could experience were you to take responsibility. If you ask me, the experience is the difference between looking out of the second floor and the fifty-second floor of the Empire State building. By itself, the scenery outside is the same, but depending on where you are you get a very different perspective.

By the same principle, let's take a second look at the questions we raised above:

- *Is my boss too intimidating, or am I not showing the courage to express my needs?*
- *Is my peer not trustworthy, or am I not collaborative enough?*
- *What would I do with respect to the culture of working late if I were not insecure?*
- *Do my team members not have the hunger to achieve, or am I unable to inspire them enough?*
- *Has my spouse stopped caring for my feelings, or have I stopped demonstrating my love to my partner?*
- *Have the kids stopped listening to us, or are we not fully capable of understanding their needs at the moment?*

Between the two alternative possibilities in each of these questions, what's your own version of reality?

Let's be real. There's probably a little bit of truth at both ends. However, hoping for the other person to change to suit you is wishful thinking. It's unlikely to happen. All the same, when you start to make the change on your side (such as, you learn to express your needs to your senior or how to inspire your team members), you start the process of altering their response towards you. Your intimidating boss will likely not change their leadership style, but they would start being more responsive to your views and needs. If you were to spend meaningful time with your children and genuinely try and understand the world through their lens, and then present ideas relevant to them without preaching your views, they would be more open to considering them.

Let me share an example of one of my coaching clients:

I had known Shekhar for some years. A highly respected professional, he was the CEO of a leading consumer durables business. At one of our meetings, he shared his concern about his team. He mentioned that among his team of nine functional directors, five were doing a great job, two were doing alright and two were underperforming. He highlighted that the last two, his directors of sales and manufacturing functions, were not very aligned with his vision. He believed that collectively the team was clearly punching below its weight. He seemed quite stressed about it and wondered what else he could do to improve the team's performance.

As we started to work together, we discussed the composition of his team and some of the specific areas that he wanted each of them to improve on. That done, I encouraged him to reflect on his own approach towards the team and his broader leadership style—*could it be that any aspects of his behaviour were coming in the way of creating an empowered and inspired team?* He also decided to seek feedback from his team on how they perceived him. Based on the feedback and his self-reflections, he identified certain facets of his leadership style that needed addressing: he tended to be very goal-oriented in his interactions and not as people-oriented; he had an intense personality and was perceived by his team members as aloof; and he easily became impatient with his colleagues and was quick to judge them.

With greater self-awareness of his approach (and some of its drawbacks), he began to consider alternative ways of leading. He started taking the time to engage with his team in more informal conversations and better understand their perspective. He also worked on his listening skills and consciously tried to make everyone feel included in discussions. Appreciating the merit of seeing the potential in everyone and not judging them too soon, he became more empathetic and started acknowledging the team members more often. To empower the team further, he made each of the directors responsible for championing one of the top projects of the company.

Within a few months, Shekhar was beginning to see the results of his changes. The team's motivation level and the quality of their contribution was improving and he personally felt much more engaged with the team.

Shekhar also became open to try new ideas with the directors of sales and manufacturing. As he examined his interactions with them closely, he could see some clear patterns there too. The sales director was new to the company. Because of Shekhar's years of experience in sales, he had been unintentionally quite domineering when sharing his views on the ongoing sales initiatives. He realised this might have been making the sales director unsure of himself. He decided to step back a bit and empower the sales director more.

Further, Shekhar noted he did not enjoy a great working relationship with the director of manufacturing. One of the reasons for this was that he was not particularly interested in manufacturing-related issues and, as a result, never actively engaged with the director or his team. As he consciously invested time in understanding the manufacturing domain and visited two of the factories with the director, he began appreciating the work being done by that team and could better respond to the director's challenges.

Shekhar felt highly energised by his progress and committed to build on it. He also started to talk to the team about the changes he had been making and encouraged them to be more self-aware and reflective. He held several formal and informal sessions with his larger team across different offices and factories to build a deeper connect with them. Six months after we finished working together, I received a really heartwarming message from Shekhar. He had just received the latest feedback report on his leadership team's engagement and motivation scores. The numbers were off the charts!

What comes in the way?

Why is it so hard for us to look within for change?
Why do we routinely fail to put it into practice?
How is it that we continue to blame other people or external circumstances for our setbacks?

There are three key reasons. First, our judgmental nature. We are severely conditioned to judging others and our circumstances. We judge our peers as overly ambitious, selfish and self-promoting; we judge our team members as lacking ownership and drive. We judge our life partner to be insensitive, moody or demanding and our children to be distracted, careless or idealistic. We blame the organisation for its work culture, politics and lack of meritocracy. These subconscious beliefs serve as rationalisation for our lack of effectiveness as a leader, life partner or a parent. However, whether they are accurate observations or not, they do not actually serve us well. They merely distract us.

Second, our ego. We are attached to an idealised image of our own self. Right from childhood, based on our own perception and the messages we receive from parents, teachers and friends, we form a mental impression of a 'perfect self'. Over time, this impression gets solidified in our psyche, and we subconsciously want to live up to it. This is the persona we like to present to the world as well. For example, you may identify yourself with being smart, successful, righteous, tough, fearless and so on. In order to preserve this self-image, you will likely resist any situation that threatens it. You may need to improve your relationship skills, but that may be in conflict with your self-image of righteousness; you may need to learn new stress-management techniques, but your identification with toughness does not allow you to; and because of your ego, you fail to pay heed to your colleagues' constructive feedback. To grow, we have to let go of our attachment to a false sense of self, our ego.

The last reason is inertia. We are all creatures of habit. Our bodies and minds are comfortable with the familiar, even though what's familiar may not be what's best for us. Whether it's our food and exercise habits, working styles, preparation routines for an important event or decision-making approaches, we usually prefer to stick to the familiar. Change is difficult. However, for us to experience real growth, we have to step out of our comfort zone. As British poet Alfred Tennyson wisely observed, 'The shell must break before the bird can fly.'

Often, you may not even realise the need for any change in your approach. Or, you may be unsure about how to go about making the changes. But even in situations where you are aware of what you need to do, you may end up not doing it. Exercise is a classic example. Everyone is aware of its benefits, but does everyone act on it? Similarly, just because you are aware of the need to be more empathetic, less temperamental or speak your mind more often, it doesn't become easy to put it into practice.

Readiness to change

Over the years, I have noticed certain characteristics shared by individuals who are good at making changes. Based on them, here are a few suggestions for you.

1. Build a growth mindset

People with a fixed mindset believe leaders are born. They operate with the premise that you either possess the required skills to be a leader or you don't. Alternately, they judge themselves on the basis of their existing capabilities and tend to believe that those are permanent and set for life. As a leader, this thought process is self-limiting and impacts their motivation to strive for higher personal goals. Further, it affects their perception of other colleagues, particularly their team members. They are more likely to assess their colleagues based on their inherent strengths and weaknesses, rather than see the latter, essentially, as opportunities for development.

Leaders with a growth mindset view work and life as a learning journey. They do not perceive lack of knowledge or capability in any area as an inherent limitation and hence do not feel threatened in such situations. They don't pretend to be smarter than they are in order to protect their ego and are willing to be vulnerable in order to learn. Besides, such leaders are more committed to develop and grow their team members—because they deeply believe the team members can.

2. Be open to feedback

A feedback loop is an essential part of any effective and evolving system. That's why successful organisations actively seek customer feedback. That's why we have the employee appraisal system in organisations. We all develop blind spots over time and if it were not for feedback, they would remain the same. That said, not all leaders are good at receiving feedback. Given their professional progress, they conveniently settle into the subconscious belief that they don't really need to change in any significant way. All the same, the ones who make the shift from good to great recognise that they need to constantly evolve to be better equipped to leading in an ever-changing environment. They routinely search for ways to enhance their skills and learn new ones.

They are particularly open to receiving feedback. Many of them *actively* seek it. They talk to their colleagues, other professional relationships, mentors as well as family members for ideas on what they can do better or differently. They are willing to be vulnerable in opening themselves for critique. They don't perceive negative feedback as criticism or take it personally. Instead, they are quick to acknowledge and thank others for providing candid feedback.

One simple exercise that my clients find helpful, particularly while working on relationship goals, is to seek feedback using the 'three things' approach. Ideally, you would engage a cross-section of your colleagues, from seniors, peers and team members, to do this exercise. Essentially, you ask them to give you honest feedback on the following three questions:

1.   *Three things I should <u>start</u> doing in order to become a more effective leader?*
2.   *Three things I should <u>stop</u> doing in order to become a more effective leader?*
3.   *Three things I should <u>continue</u> doing in order to become a more effective leader?*

Instead of asking colleagues more broadly about how they experience you or what their suggestions are for your development, this approach forces them to give very pointed inputs. Besides, you get rich feedback in an easy and quick way. If you have six to eight colleagues providing you this feedback, you would quickly get fifty-four to seventy-two data points to reflect on and learn from.

You could do this exercise in your personal life too, by asking your family members for their feedback. To make it fun, you could even consider having each family member give feedback to everyone else. You may be surprised on the kind of specific and thoughtful feedback you get from family members, especially from your children.

3. Take responsibility for your journey of change

In an organisational setting, far too often, employees and even those in leadership positions expect the organisation to determine the kind of developmental support they receive. If you are keen to improve, you should be the one driving that agenda. You should be the one seeking out all possible help within or outside the organisation. Whether you need to attend a leadership effectiveness program, join a specific skill training, hire an executive coach or have a mentor, the responsibility to drive that initiative lies with you.

Any elite performer gets to their position with help and support. Pro tennis player Roger Federer has not one but two full-time coaches. He also has a fitness trainer and a physiotherapist. Besides, his wife, Mirka, a former professional tennis player herself, has had a significant influence on Federer's professional journey. Needless to say, without the support of each of these experts, he wouldn't be where he is. Seeking help does not diminish you in any way; it only reflects your commitment to personal growth and better sets you up for success.

The deepest learning is self-directed. While attending leadership programmes or reading management books can be inspiring, ultimately you have to commit to yourself to bring the new learning into your life. Only when you put the new ideas into practice, will they become a part of the new you. When you take ownership of your journey of change, you hold yourself accountable for your progress. Not only are you likelier to meet better results, but you also increase your chances of sustaining those results.

Personal actions

1. What kind of mindset (growth or fixed) do you currently have? How open are you to feedback? How often do you tend to externalise your challenges?
2. What are some of your greatest challenges at work or in life currently? (You may have identified these at the end of the first chapter.)
3. What do you need to change within yourself to overcome these challenges?
4. How ready are you to commit yourself to working on these changes?
5. What needs to shift for you to strengthen your readiness for change?

Insight 3

From Busyness to Thoughtfulness

Until you make the unconscious conscious,
it will direct your life and you will call it fate.
— CARL JUNG, Swiss psychiatrist and psychotherapist

IF YOU ARE A LEADER IN ANY CAPACITY, WHETHER OF A MULTINATIONAL organisation, a small- to mid-sized business or a public- or a social-sector institution, chances are that you are invariably busy. You routinely work with tight deadlines, have significant travel commitments, important presentations to make and stiff targets to accomplish. If you are based in a big city, it's likely that you live a fast-paced life. The pressure to stay connected 24/7 and the compulsion to respond to emails and WhatsApp messages in record time makes it worse. Unfortunately, in this busyness of life, there's no time to pause and reflect.

Leaders who start on the journey of positive change, with a goal to move towards great leadership, consciously create structured time for reflection in their life. Just as you need regular exercise for your physical health, you also need reflection time for your emotional and mental well-being.

Actively reflecting is different from thinking. Most leaders' thinking ability is exceptionally developed—they are smart and can think well. However, a large part of that thinking happens in an automated and conditioned way. If you react negatively to bad news, chances are you will always have negative thoughts in response to such news; if you are driven by aggressive sales targets, you will be hard-pressed to approach any sales situation differently; if you don't like one of your peers, your instinctive response will always be one of envy and marked by the desire to prove them wrong. The challenge leaders face is not that they don't think enough, it's that they think too much and often in the same conditioned way.

Creating pauses for reflection helps you feel more centred and allows you to take a step back and view the same situation from a fresh perspective. Reflection forces you to slow down your conditioned flow of thoughts and respond to a situation in a more balanced manner. It helps you operate from a place of being more present to the immediate reality than react based on the baggage of conditioned thoughts and beliefs. You are also more likely to be creative: people often get their most insightful ideas when they are physically and mentally relaxed— while walking in nature, listening to music, resting in bed, in the shower or playing with children. Such pauses give meaning to the rest of our pursuits. Only when we add spaces to letters, do they become words; it's the pauses between sounds that make them music.

Reflection helps us deepen many aspects of our self-awareness that are crucial to how we live and lead. Unless we have a deeper understanding of ourselves, we are easily influenced by what's popular around us. As the Chinese philosopher Lao Tzu said, 'He who knows others is learned, he who knows himself is wise.' This enhanced awareness relates to all aspects of our being—the physical, emotional, mental and spiritual.

Physical being

On the physical level, regular and structured reflection can help you observe and become aware of your physical habits and being. You can learn to pay attention to your physical health and your eating, exercising and sleeping habits. You may become better equipped to notice the subtle shifts in your energy levels during the day and discover what might be causing such shifts—for example, workload, diet or stressful conversations.

Besides, you would start to notice how you tend to spend your time and why. What's the ratio of your time spent on long-term planning versus working out your short-term goals? How much time do you spend with the family or pursuing a fulfilling interest? How many hours in a day do you spend on emails, messages and social media? Recently, a client of mine downloaded an app to track his phone habits and found that, on an average, he picked up his phone 180 times and checked his emails 130 times daily. Tells you something about yourself, doesn't it? Time is precious for busy leaders, and becoming mindful of the connection between different activities and the time you spend towards those can be extremely revealing (more about that in Insight 4).

Emotional being

As you start to step away, consciously and consistently, from your busyness, you also begin to notice your emotional being. You begin to recognise your recurring feelings and what causes them. For example, is your state of emotional being directly linked to how well you are meeting your targets at work? Do you routinely get anxious about your year-end performance rating, particularly compared to your peers? Do you feel hurt every time one of your colleagues passes a critical comment?

Furthermore, you may learn more about your emotional make-up. How do you deal with setbacks? How resilient are you? Do you tend to brood over failures or find it easy to move on? Are you quick to point fingers at others, or do you tend to blame yourself and feel guilty? As you learn about these aspects, you may begin to realise how stress-prone you are. Many a time, the leaders I am working with associate their high stress levels with their work pressures. They see stress as temporary and consider it the outcome of a topical challenge—the prevailing business environment, the current lack of resources in the team, their recent role expansion and so forth. However, as they practise reflection, some realise that their stress levels have continually been high. They recognise that there's always some external reason that can be pinpointed as the source of their high levels of stress at any point of time. Naturally, the antidotes they need for their stress, then, are different from what they may have originally envisaged.

Through regular reflection, you may also become more aware of how you relate to others. How easily do you get along with people? What kind of colleagues do you find it challenging to collaborate with? How perceptive are you of others' feelings and their emotional make-up? How often do you judge people based on some of their personality traits? We'll explore more about emotional well-being and effective relationships in the section on 'Applying the *Inside-Out* Approach: Heart'.

Mental being

Creating regular breaks for your busy mind allows you to see your own thought processes in a new light. As you observe your recurring mental patterns, you become conscious of your attitudes, biases and deeply held beliefs and how they dictate your behaviour. You may become aware of your unconscious need to win or be right every time, or the need to be liked by others around you and how that inadvertently makes you avoid any confrontation, or your fear of making mistakes and how that makes you more controlling of your team. You may start to notice your bias for action and how that might be impacting the ability of your team to focus on actual priorities, or your tendency to judge colleagues based on their short-term performance and how that shapes the type of responsibilities you offer them.

Through reflection, every detail of how we live becomes more pronounced, as if processed through slow motion action replay, and as we choose to slow down from our hectic and goal-driven life, our subconscious triggers become amplified and more easily perceptible. We start to see our propensity to identify with our work, our job titles and the material benefits they bring. We also begin to appreciate how such identification dictates the lack of our work-life balance.

Reflection brings to light how we frequently put our current happiness on hold, making it rely too heavily on future events like becoming 'more successful' or 'having more money'. With higher self-awareness, we realise that to experience real contentment, we must learn to be happy in the present, despite the perceived imperfections of current life situations.

Spiritual being

Once you detach yourself from the adrenaline rush of a fast-paced life, you pave the way to examine key existential questions related to your work and life, including your core values, life purpose and true identity.

Have you ever asked yourself what your core values are and how well your life is aligned to them? Busyness, coupled with the strong influences of our social environment, can result in losing connection with our inner values. An inability to live your core values silently and gradually contributes to unhappiness and a feeling of a lack of fulfilment. For example, if you're someone who deeply values integrity, slowly adapting to an environment that sometimes encourages cutting corners for achieving results would leave you feeling conflicted within. Sadly, as you get accustomed to the new way of operating, you may not easily recognise the source of your nagging discomfort. Quiet moments of reflection automatically bring such nuances to your conscious awareness.

Similarly, stepping off the treadmill of activity may enable you to examine and resolve the deeper purpose of your life. As you create distance from your maddening pace, you question the core objective of your daily pursuits. What's the real point of this frantic race to achieve more, more and more? What's the relevance of your actions and professional work to society? While we will discuss this theme in greater detail in Insight 12, let me highlight one key aspect here.

In the beginning, such seemingly nagging questions can feel like a distraction from your goals and plans. However, if you continue to question the meaning behind your pursuit of bigger, better and more materialistic progress—which, by the way, is not necessarily wrong in its own sense—you'll find this exercise is extremely liberating. You start to identify what's central to your life, what is it that you, deep down, really want your life and work to be about. It will also help you notice things that are superfluous but have been eating up a lot of your time and energy. Building such clarity can significantly sharpen your focus, productivity and fulfilment as a leader.

As you build your practice, structured reflection time can give you an insight into the very core of your being, leading you to who you are and what your true identity is amidst all the roles you play in life. It is not unusual for busy executives to get so consumed by their work and the little self-centred battles that go with it that they lose sight of the bigger picture—not of their work, but of their life. Becoming aware of your spiritual identity unites you with your innate nature and reminds you of your interconnectedness with everything else in the universe. And that, I promise, will have a calming and anchoring effect on you.

How to reflect

By three methods we may learn wisdom: first, by reflection, which is noblest; second, by imitation, which is easiest; and third, by experience, which is the most bitter.

– CONFUCIUS, Chinese philosopher

You can inculcate the habit of reflection in your lifestyle in a number of ways. I have personally found the practice of meditation a particularly powerful means to do so. The word 'meditation' originated from the Latin word 'meditatio', which means contemplation. It generally involves engaging in a mental exercise directed at reaching a deeper state of focus, awareness and relaxation. Staying focused on something specific, like the breath, enables us to slowly disengage from our recurring and conditioned thought patterns. Meditation requires us to be in an open and accepting state, where we don't judge our thoughts or our inability to let go of them. This leads to the quietening of the mind. That, in turn, results in a relaxed mental state that is open to engaging with reality without fear, greed or any other emotional attachment.

Extensive research, including that undertaken by Harvard Medical School and the American National Institute of Health, conducted with practitioners of transcendental meditation and mindfulness meditation, shows that meditation is helpful in a multitude of ways. It is proven to reduce anxiety, stress and chronic pain, strengthen the immune system and improve sleep quality. It is reported to be helpful with enhancing self-esteem, tolerance, positive emotions, emotional resilience and quality of relationships. Studies show that sustained practice of meditation helps executives build greater foresight, clearer thinking, creativity, authentic relationships and higher productivity. It develops leaders' self-awareness at all the four levels of being that we discussed earlier. Consequently, leaders who practise meditation are more confident, purposeful, resilient and happier, and better equipped to produce impactful and sustainable results.

Meditation techniques abound. In fact, there are almost too many, and if you are just starting out, the choice can be overwhelming. If you are familiar with a specific technique or know someone who's benefitted from one, consider starting with that. As you gain more direct exposure of the practice, your personal experience can guide you with your choices. Then, you can choose to either persevere with the same practice or learn another one. You can also consider exploring well-known techniques like transcendental meditation and vipassana. Besides, many meditation apps are available these days, Headspace and Calm being two of the most popular. Do your research and assess what you feel most drawn to.

Alternatively, you can consider writing a journal as a way to incorporate a practice of conscious reflection. Articulating your thoughts on a piece of paper is a powerful processing tool, as it forces you to give shape to otherwise abstract thoughts about various issues. It thus automatically helps clarify many things. Writing also gives some degree of finality and closure to reflection. You can record the questions you wish to ponder over and make a note of your thoughts on a regular basis. You can also make a daily note of your dominant thoughts and feelings of the day—this can be reflective and therapeutic. For journaling to be effective though, it is important that you don't judge yourself, your thoughts or your feelings. Many a time, we grasp an insight or a new approach, but over time miss out on fully incorporating it in our life. A journal is useful in this regard. A ready archive of entries, a journal can help you build reference points as a reminder of the journey you're on.

Lastly, inculcating a reading habit is very supportive of a reflection practice. Reading thoughtful books in the genre of personal growth, including in the fields of psychology, philosophy and spirituality, can serve as a regular reminder of some of the insights you may have gained during your own personal reflections. These reminders urge you to stay connected with and put those insights into practice. Listening to inspirational podcasts and talks can serve a similar purpose.

Reflection is not an occasional event but an ongoing practice. It's a way of life. Some clients of mine like to think of structured reflection as analogous to the idea of a power nap—short, concentrated and yet potent. They commit to a focused time, of generally around ten minutes every day, which is dedicated to reflection. It could be early in the morning, last thing at night, first thing at work or during their commute to or from work. They stick to their plan religiously, and yet these precious moments do not necessarily interfere with their daily routines.

When done consistently, reflection has the potential to accelerate your growth, create a cycle of self-improvement and enrich your experiences. Every step of progress is an occasion to assess what worked well for you and every setback an opportunity to learn what you could have done better. In that regard, building a discipline of regular reflection, almost as a part of your daily or weekly routine, can be empowering.

Personal actions

1. How would you rate your level of self-awareness across the four dimensions (physical, emotional, mental and spiritual)? Which aspects do you need to pay more attention to?
2. Do you have a structured reflection practice in place? If yes, what has been your experience with it? If not, where will you start?
3. What, specifically, do you need to start doing towards building a healthy reflection practice?

Applying the *Inside-Out* Approach: Impact

Insight 4

From Delivering Results to Making an Impact

Do not follow where the path may lead.
Go instead where there is no path and leave a trail.
— Ralph Waldo Emerson, American essayist and poet

DO YOU OFTEN GET FEEDBACK THAT, AS A LEADER, YOU ARE DELIVERING great results, but not making enough impact? Do you feel that despite your performance, you run the risk of being overlooked for a promotion? Are you running out of ideas to get noticed and be counted?

You are not alone. I have the privilege of working with some of the most successful leaders on an everyday basis. Some of them have been in leadership positions for a long time, while others are relatively new to it. Many of them confess that they're experiencing at least one of the above scenarios.

One of the key roles you play as a leader is making a positive impact in your domain, both within the organisation and outside, in the industry and, hopefully, in the wider society. It is very possible that the skills that helped you reach your current level of success may not necessarily help you get to the next. Leadership calls for making a lasting contribution to the business, industry or the field you are involved in. Such contributions include bringing to the table thought leadership, creative and innovative solutions and long-term initiatives—in short, adding value to the organisation in areas beyond your defined role. It includes making a difference to the lives of people who are, directly or indirectly, part of your organisation: employees, families, clients and the broader communities your work touches.

Making an impact is closely related to making strategic contributions. Delivering steady results in your defined role, while important by itself, hardly qualifies for that. Say, you are a business leader and deliver healthy financial results for the year. That is a positive achievement, yet it does not necessarily move the organisation forward or fundamentally improve the way your business or industry is run. If you lead an NGO and routinely meet your internal evaluation metric for the services you provide to the society, it's great and truly meaningful. All the same, if you want to make a significant impact in your sector, you may want to consider influencing public opinion, governmental policies and other action groups towards shifting the awareness, perception and funding for your sector.

In that context, here are some ideas for you to consider so your work can be more impactful, allowing you to fulfil your personal potential and get recognised with all the rewards you deserve.

Identify three things that matter

Firstly, if you want to leave more of an impact, you'll need to become more strategic in your approach and get comfortable with letting go of the temptation to get overly involved in the details of operations. You have to be able to look at the big picture of your landscape and identify a handful of priorities—the ones that would make the greatest difference to the quality of your contribution over an extended period of time. If you are in a middle to senior management role, you can consider this time period to be twelve-eighteen months, whereas in more senior roles, you can look at three-five years.

As you create a list, I recommend you limit your focus to three priorities. My experience suggests that working with three is generally the most productive approach: a list of three is small enough for you to pay meaningful attention to each priority and yet big enough that the outcomes are significant. While considering these priorities, think transformational, not transactional—not of the processes but of structures; not of your annual goals but of the long-term mission of the organisation; not of your organisation alone but of the whole ecosystem it operates in.

Here are some examples. These are indicative of the priorities generally applicable to the top leadership of an organisation. Based on the scope of your role, you can adapt them to suit your personal context.

- Bring about a digital transformation of the organisation.
- Reduce the organisation's carbon footprint by 50 per cent.
- Influence industrial policy to create a better, level playing field.
- Identify and prepare the business head's successor.
- Hire, organise and develop a high-performing leadership team.
- Build three strategic alliances to create competitive advantage for the organisation.
- Launch two new innovations to dominate the market.
- Diversify the network of suppliers to protect the organisation from overdependence in a future crisis.
- Create an advocacy group to better fulfil the mission of the not-for-profit organisation.

Furthermore, besides being strategic in choosing priorities and implementing them, impactful leaders have a strategic outlook towards life in general. They tend to view the bigger picture in every situation or engagement. Here's an example of what I mean. After a presentation on a significant new initiative, I typically notice two types of responses from leaders in the room. There are those who express their concern about things like the scope of the initiative, the tight deadlines and resource constraints—the *what* and *how* of it. Then, there are others who question how well the initiative aligns with the group's long-term objectives—the *why* of it. If you naturally gravitate to the former, consider adopting the latter approach to every interaction you have with seniors, peers or team members—pay attention to the underlying strategic issue you are trying to address and the longer-term impact of your present actions.

Disciplined time-management

Great leaders know time is precious, and they are masters at managing it. They are adept at prioritising their activities and ruthless in focusing on the things that really matter.

To start with, think about the percentage of your time you would need to dedicate towards your top priorities for you to do justice to them. The most impactful leaders spend upwards of two-thirds of their time on these priorities. On the other hand, when asked about the percentage of time they spend on their top priorities, leaders who are falling short in the quality of their impact respond that it's anywhere between 20 to 35 per cent. Can you see the difference?

Now, my intention here is not to extend your working hours, but to make adjustments to them in a way that you are able to create time for your top priorities. I have found a simple tool that helps leaders gain insights into how they are managing their time and priorities: Stephen Covey's time-management grid. You may have come across it in the past, but if you find managing your time a challenge, I would recommend you try it.

The four quadrants in the following diagram are self-explanatory. To analyse how you spend your time, I would suggest you record each of your activities, along with the time you spent on it, in this grid. Whether you are busy with meetings, projects, emails or reviews, record everything—suitably slotted in the quadrant where it belongs. Do this on a daily basis for a fortnight. Please be mindful that the fortnight

Stephen Covey's time management grid

	URGENT	NOT URGENT
IMPORTANT	ACTIVITIES I Crisis Pressing Problems Deadline-driven projects Production problems	ACTIVITIES II Prevention Relationship Building Recognising new opportunities Planning Recreation Production capability problems
NOT IMPORTANT	ACTIVITIES III Interruptions, some calls Some emails, some reports Some meetings Popular activities Pressing matters	ACTIVITIES IV Trivia, busy work Some emails Some phone calls Time wasters Pleasent activities

you choose is one that's broadly representative of your schedule and not one that's abnormal because of any unusual activities or one-off commitments. Once you have all the entries, calculate the percentage of time you are spending in each of the quadrants.

This is usually quite revealing. Clearly, in leadership positions, you want to have a sizeable proportion of your time going towards the important, not urgent category—quadrant II activities. These are ones that support you in making an impact. For example, in your personal life, regular exercise is not an urgent activity, but it's important. If you skip it for a few days, it's not the end of the world, but sticking to an exercise discipline is important for your health in the long run. Also, when you don't attend to quadrant II activities in a timely fashion, they become quadrant I activities. Many of the stressful deadlines that show up in quadrant I do so because you didn't plan enough for them at an early stage. Generally speaking, you can reduce the time spent in quadrant III by delegating many of those activities. You surely want to limit or eliminate the time spent in quadrant IV.

In order to manifest your top priorities or other quadrant II-type activities into reality, and to avoid the risk of being consumed by short-term goals, create non-negotiable time windows upfront in your calendar on a weekly basis. You need to ensure that you single-mindedly dedicate this time to your top priorities, without the temptation to check emails or take calls. This approach will set you up for becoming more impactful. You can choose, say, to break down your key strategic priorities for eighteen months into measurable activities that you can focus on in the coming weeks and months. If, for instance, your intention is to launch two innovative products or services in the next eighteen months, you will want to plan time in the first three months for activities like promoting the idea with your research team, arriving at a long list of ideas, creating a proposal, getting buy-in and budget approvals for initiating work and so on. Similarly, you can schedule specific aspects of these activities in the coming weeks so you stay on track for your monthly and quarterly milestones.

Mastering the delegation paradigm

Impactful leaders are highly skilled at delegation. To be able to focus on your top priorities, it is imperative that you have a strong delegation muscle. Most leaders recognise the importance of delegation, but not everyone is good at it. Because here's the thing . . . even leaders who generally consider themselves good at delegation tend to delegate what they *can't* do—not what they *lack competence in*, but what they don't have time for, the overflow of their work. Leaders who are exceptional at delegation follow a different paradigm altogether. *They don't delegate what they can't do; they do only what no one else can.*

That's a very different mindset. Whatever work flows to them, their first instinct is to determine who in their team is best suited to do it. That ensures that most of the business-as-usual stuff is attended to by the team, leaving the leader to focus primarily on the big-ticket agenda. Besides freeing up your time, this is empowering for your team as well.

A common reason leaders share with me for not delegating aggressively is that their team members are not responsible or reliable enough—that they have tried delegating but in the end they still need to do most of the work themselves. I believe that the team members' readiness is limited by the imagination of their leaders. This is true of parenting too—the child's potential is limited by the imagination of the parents. Surprisingly, not delegating enough or choosing to take on more than you should is the easier option, but it's also the more expensive one.

While we will explore in greater detail how you can coach your team towards higher performance in Insight 6, a tool I recommend to my clients and that can support you in developing a clear delegation structure is the 'Delegation Tree'. As Susan Scott recommends in *Fierce Conversations*, drawing a parallel to a tree, all decisions that team members typically have to make can be divided into four categories—namely, 'Leaf', 'Branch', 'Trunk' and 'Root'. The category of 'Leaf' represents areas where team members can independently make a decision, act on it and don't have to inform you about it. 'Branch' includes decisions where team members can independently make the decision and act on it, but need to keep you posted at an agreed frequency. 'Trunk' decisions are those where the team members can do all the prep work and make up their minds, but need to check with you before pulling the trigger. Finally, 'Root' captures decisions that have the greatest long-term implications and must be made with deliberate consultations with you, as the leader. Such a structure can support you in communicating your expectations and approach to your team members in a clear manner. Over time, hopefully, you and your team can move more of the decisions from the 'Root' and 'Trunk' categories to the 'Leaf' and 'Branch' categories. When that starts to happen, know that you're successfully empowering your team to tap into their full potential and are setting yourself up for making greater impact.

Embracing personality shifts

Staying focused on strategic priorities and delegating effectively requires certain deeper personality shifts. Specifically, it entails cultivating three key personality traits—not seeking perfection, cultivating a willingness to let go and learning to say no.

Perfectionism is revered in organisations, particularly at junior and middle management levels. It allows seniors to confidently rely on you. However, the same trait becomes a drag in leadership positions. There's a key difference between a manager and a leader. As Warren Bennis of The Leadership Institute at the University of Southern California states, 'Managers do things right, leaders do the right things.' Impactful leaders focus on issues, projects and pursuits that make a significant difference. Although they can surely turn out perfect results, they choose not to pay undue attention to perfecting all the details for everything. They recognise that all the work that passes their desk doesn't need to be 'platinum' standard; they are comfortable with letting some things be at a 'gold' standard, and some at even a 'silver' standard.

This requires learning to let go. Delegating to others, who may not produce work at exactly the same level of perfection as you, tests your ability to let go of your rigid expectations. It requires you to become more flexible. In the spirit of letting go, you'd do well to also review what you can stop doing or get less involved in. Imagine a hypothetical personal crisis that requires your attention and leaves you with no choice but to delegate work. What three things would you stop doing? Do you have to personally attend all the meetings and calls that you currently attend; can someone else in your team attend some of them? What about being less restless about your unfinished to-do list and persistently following up with your colleagues? As management guru Peter Drucker says, 'Half the leaders I've met don't need to learn what to start doing, but what to stop.' What can you stop doing? How about initiating that now?

To equip yourself to be effective at managing your priorities and time, particularly if you tend to be permissive and accommodating by nature, it's worth your time to learn to say 'No'. You have to say 'No' to meetings or calls you don't need to attend—and most organisations have plenty of those. You have to choose to push back seniors and other colleagues when they make unreasonable demands on your time.

As head of business strategy at a large e-retailer, Sonia took pride in being a highly approachable leader. Sonia was well liked. Members of her team freely walked into her office to chat about issues they wanted to resolve with her. This would happen several times a day. As Sonia paid greater attention to being more impactful in her role, she became aware of the limitations of her open-door policy. While it empowered her team to be in active communication with her and not slow down on any issues, it held her back from focusing on strategic issues that required her greater undivided attention.

She decided to become better organised. She also spoke to her team to get better organised themselves in how they approached her. She decided to have a forty-five minute meeting with each of her four direct reports on a fixed day and time of the week. She would review all updates and discuss any outstanding issues that they had. The team members were free to talk to her during the week, but needed to set up a time with her assistant. This forced them to be more structured and organised and allowed Sonia to be more effective.

Consistent Messaging

While working through the above approaches should put you in a stronger position to make an impact, if you are the type who is uncomfortable with messaging your ideas or progress to your wider stakeholder network, it can hold you back. This is particularly relevant in the Asian context, where 'content' is considered supreme, and 'form' is almost looked down upon. Many of the leaders I work with in the region have grown up with a strong value system that suggests that you should just focus on doing your job well and others will eventually recognise you for it.

While this is a very thoughtful approach, and I have personally grown up with it, not communicating your ideas, plans and achievements to a relevant audience might be delimiting. I am not for once suggesting that you should move to other extreme, where you spend more time talking about your work than doing it. However, do explore if there's an opportunity for you to achieve a better balance. Instead of focusing 100 per cent on the doing and nearly zero on the communicating, how about an 85:15 combination?

As Steuart Henderson of the Department of Psychology at George Washington University observes, 'Doing business without advertising is like winking at a girl in the dark. You know what you are doing but nobody else does.' Just as organisations, even the most successful ones, need to advertise, leaders need to actively talk about their ideas and actions to their stakeholder network. This is important because without active communication, your work and contribution may go unnoticed. Besides, as you make more stakeholders aware of the impact you and your team are making, you increase your chances of getting more resources for your future initiatives.

Like with advertising, it is also important that you persist with communicating a consistent message. Specifically, as you pursue your top priorities, actively talk about them through the journey. You need to share your thoughts with the relevant people, whether board members, senior leadership or other colleagues, right from the planning stage. Discuss your progress on these initiatives during the key reviews and updates. Finally, upon completion, communicate the achievement of your objectives and the key learnings from the initiative. This consistent messaging helps engage the various stakeholders in your journey as well as builds a strong association between the key initiatives and you.

Lastly, many leaders share that they are not particularly adept at engaging with super seniors whom they don't meet very often. I recommend preparing three types of messaging around your priorities to suit the different types of interactions you may have, especially if you are not a natural conversationalist. Firstly, have an elevator pitch ready. This is a two-minute message about one of your top priorities, one that you can use when someone very senior simply asks you, *'How's it going?'* Instead of rambling on about how you may have been busy the previous week, which they are unlikely to be interested in, talk about your top priority for the year. A statement like, *'There's a lot going on in my division, but what I am most excited about working on this year is . . . state your top priority, e.g. making our HR team ready to support our aggressive expansion plans,'* will make a strong impact and surely evoke interest from the listener.

Similarly, prepare talking points for a ten-minute message that covers the headlines of your top priorities. The more senior the leader you are interacting with, the greater the emphasis on keeping your comments to the strategic issues needs to be. Thirdly, for a longer meeting, say over coffee or lunch, be prepared with an expanded description of your priorities. For someone who's interested in your work, you should be ready to talk not only about your priorities, but also why they are important to the organisation, how you are progressing on them, what challenges you are facing and what you are learning from the process.

External connects

A common trait I notice among leaders of large organisations is the tendency to be inward-looking. As you grow in any organisation and manage more complex roles within larger teams, there's just so much going on that it is easy to get consumed by the sheer pace of organisational goals and activities. What tends to not get sufficient, or *any*, attention in the process is the necessity of staying connected with peers outside the organisation. The peers you connect with externally do not have to be limited to executives from your industry. Consider staying in touch with peers from other industries as well. Meeting people from diverse industries and learning about their world expands our mind. We gain different perspectives to solve our current challenges in new ways. How is an IT firm dealing with the challenge of attracting talent? What's a large retailer doing to enhance customer service? What organisational structure and approaches does a start-up have to encourage innovation? Responses to these are likely to be relevant to you and your organisation irrespective of whether you are an investment bank, a consumer business or an NGO. As you do this on a steady basis (maybe one such lunch meeting every month), you strengthen your capacity to make an impact. You can also consider attending relevant conferences and speaking at industry forums. Besides learning from others, these also offer you a platform to showcase your experiences. As a side note, anecdotally speaking, leaders with strong external networks tend to be valued and even paid more!

Personal actions

1. What are your top three strategic priorities for the next twelve–eighteen months (or longer)? What percentage of your time do you spend on these at present? Ideally, what percentage of time would you like to invest in these? What needs to change for this to happen?

2. Complete the Covey time-management grid to determine what percentage of time you spend in each of the four quadrants. What opportunities do you see here? What needs to change for you to increase the time you spend in quadrant II? How can you create more non-negotiable time windows in your calendar towards these activities?

3. How well would your team say you delegate? What can you start doing to empower your team more? What three things can you stop doing?

4. How good are you at engaging with senior-most leaders? Would crafting an elevator pitch and other messaging ideas help?

5. What opportunities do you see for connecting more actively with peers, friends and acquaintances from diverse industries? How can you approach it?

Applying the *Inside-Out* Approach: Heart

Insight 5

From Being Aggressive or Permissive to Assertive and Authentic

He who conquers others is strong; he who conquers himself is mighty.

– LAO TZU, Chinese philosopher

IT'S NOT WHAT HAPPENS TO US, IT'S HOW WE RELATE TO IT THAT MATTERS. Change is within us—in order to alter our connection with any challenging situation, we just need to be willing to look within.

This is truer in our relationships than anywhere else, and a major part of leadership comprises engaging, influencing, convincing and motivating others. The higher you go up the corporate ladder, the lower your *direct personal* contribution to the overall results. Instead, you need to build deep relationships with your internal colleagues—your team, peers and seniors. Besides, depending upon your specific leadership role, you are perhaps required to build effective external relationships with business partners, clients, distributors, board members, investors and regulators.

Yet, only a minority of leaders thrive in building and nurturing quality relationships. Naturally, there are a number of factors that influence our ability to form such relationships, but let's take a closer look at one aspect that I see crop up way too often.

Our childhood experiences, coupled with our genetic makeup, significantly influence our emotional make-up as adults. Our sense of self-esteem, temperament, perceptiveness, relationship skills and ability to give and receive love are directly impacted by these factors.

Based on different combinations of these attributes, there are any number of distinct personality types possible. While we will discuss these in Insight 10, let's examine two specific personality types here, namely *aggressive* and *permissive*—a vast majority of leaders fall into one of these two categories, even though they might at varying positions on the spectrum.

The 'aggressive' type

The 'aggressive' type tends to possess high self-confidence, their confidence sometimes being arguably higher than their actual abilities. They generally believe that they are in the right and are confident in freely expressing their point of view. While they have great respect for themselves, they tend to have lesser respect and empathy towards others. They are likely to consider others to be less competent. For them, the sources of problems are always external. Not inclined to look within, they operate from the instinct that it's generally someone else who's at fault, and not them.

This type tends to be more vocal, louder and pushy in their approach. They generally like to get their way and can be dominating in a relationship. This can even spill into a sense of entitlement—the belief that the world owes it to them. They are inclined to set rules of engagement for their colleagues in a more autocratic fashion. Besides, they are likely to deal with any transgression or underperformance from others in a strong and punishing manner.

The 'permissive' type

The 'permissive' type tends to be reserved, introverted and uncomfortable with any form of confrontation. They have a propensity to be accommodating. They also have a strong fear of rejection. In order to avoid the risk of not being liked, they would rather conform than confront. To minimise the chances of being wrong, they are unlikely to fully speak their mind and are prone to suppressing their true thoughts and feelings. For them, the need to maintain harmony in a relationship supersedes the need for honesty and arriving at the best solution. They easily give in to an argument and usually find it hard to say no to requests from colleagues.

Many leaders with a permissive personality tend to be sensitive individuals. They are sensitive to others' feelings and will generally not say anything that may be hurtful or 'rock the boat'. At the same time, they are sensitive to any form of critical feedback and can get hurt easily.

More often than not, such personality types are inward-looking and take to self-blame easily. On experiencing any setback, they are quick to judge and blame themselves for their situation. They then withdraw from the situation and may brood over it for a long time. This feeds into their subliminal belief of being a 'victim'—that others do not care for their emotions and that they are routinely left alone to fend for themselves.

However, these suppressed emotions of frustration and disappointment eventually do get released, either in passive-aggressive behaviour or in the form of sudden bursts of anger. To others, these bursts are usually unexplainable, as the immediate trigger is generally somewhat insignificant. Some of these factors make it challenging for such individuals to have deep and honest relationships—in fact, many of them have difficulty with intimacy, lest their 'true selves' be discovered.

While *aggressive* personalities are better at receiving support (they 'deserve' it), *permissive* types are more comfortable sacrificing and giving (so they are well liked).

Leadership challenges

If there were only two types of people in the world—*aggressive* or *permissive*—which one would you say you are? Of course, there is a wide spectrum, from extremely permissive and mildly permissive to mildly aggressive and extremely aggressive. Moreover, individuals may display aspects of the two types in different circumstances. However, all of us do have a dominant side, our instinctive preference.

Unfortunately, operating from either of these conditioned patterns doesn't serve any of us well. The *aggressive* type, while they may succeed in pushing through their agenda, carry the risk of being less likeable. Their peers may not be particularly collaborative if they dislike them, and team members may find them intimidating. The team may operate out of fear, hesitate to express their ideas fully and avoid sharing bad news.

The *permissive* type run the risk of not expressing their point of view fully, and as a result, limit the impact they are capable of making. Besides, their uneasiness with expressing their inner feelings to their seniors or peers leads to their own needs not being met. They avoid mature and honest discussions, which invariably results in suboptimal outcomes. They may also find it challenging to hold people accountable and are uncomfortable calling out underperformers in their team. They can be slow to give them direct and quality feedback and take appropriate action where need be.

Besides, these personality traits leave negative residual emotions within the leaders' psyche. Being aggressive makes a person impatient and prone to anger. Likewise, permissive behaviour creates a recurring feeling of inadequacy within. Such personality types fret over missed opportunities to express themselves and feel frustrated when their colleagues' ideas are well received.

Moreover, you are one whole person. Whether you are aggressive or permissive at work, that's exactly how you are with your spouse, children or friends. In fact, these traits are most pronounced in our closest relationships.

The way to be

However deep-seated these personality traits may seem, it is possible for you to break free from them. You do not have to be on either side, whether aggressive or permissive. Instead, you can learn to be *assertive* and *authentic*. In the spectrum of aggressive to permissive, this is precious middle ground—not as a compromise, but a healthy possibility.

Being *assertive* in our interactions suggests that we have a high regard for both others and ourselves. In this state, we are self-confident but not arrogant; we are firm but polite; we have a clear point of view, but are equally respectful of others' point of view; we are sensitive that we don't hurt someone else's feelings, but are fearless and *authentic* in expressing our own. In this approach to interactions, neither do we take the other person for granted nor do we let others take us for granted; we are equally comfortable in receiving help and providing support. Unlike the emotional drama that accompanies *aggressive* (feeling impatient or angry) or *permissive* (feeling victimised or disengaged) styles, *assertive* and *authentic* conversations are direct, open, mature and honest.

You may feel, 'Isn't it authentic to show my anger or frustration when one of my colleagues doesn't deliver in line with what they had promised?' Not really. Being authentic doesn't mean expressing ourselves in a manner that is unhealthy, hurtful or insensitive to the other person. Yet, you do want to show your disappointment to your colleague. An assertive approach is to first calmly listen and understand the reasons why your colleague was unable to meet his plan. Be empathetic to his situation. Assuming his reasons are not convincing enough, then, in an open and direct way, highlight to your colleague that you are disappointed with the output. There's a marked difference between expressing your disappointment with the output and the person. The former achieves the objective without making it personal. Simultaneously, engage him in a discussion on what he needs to do differently to meet his plans. In this way, you share your views clearly and hold the person accountable, but without any negative display of emotions. You don't use fear as a means to motivate your colleague, but are supportive in a coach-like manner that is more empathetic and nurturing to your colleague.

The other question that leaders have is, 'If I am not aggressive with poor performance, how will that colleague change?' Being aggressive does not change your colleague in any way. Depending on their personality type, they either become fearful (permissive) or rebellious (aggressive). While your approach may show you some results in the short-term, they will not come from a place of intrinsic motivation. Hence, this strategy is not sustainable. An assertive and authentic approach, on the other hand—irrespective of your colleague's personality—brings about a shift in how they relate and respond to you. When you provide feedback in an assertive, direct, honest and supportive way, not only will your colleagues respond positively, but they will also respect you more for it.

When you shift from aggressive or permissive to an assertive approach, you facilitate your team members to move towards the assertive and authentic space too. When you tone down your aggressive side, the permissive types in your team feel safe to express themselves. When you overcome your permissive instincts and hold your team members accountable, those with more of an aggressive personality among them begin to conform.

Making the shift

Making this shift requires working on ourselves with the belief that the change is within us. It requires a recognition that rather than blaming others or wishing for them to change, we have to change how we are engaging with the people and situations around us, and that when we change our approach, we will experience the same people and circumstances differently.

Once again, only when we choose to reflect on our habitual patterns, bringing them into our active awareness, and focus on dealing with them, do we start the process of real change. Observe yourself and establish whether being aggressive or permissive is your dominant style, particularly within your key relationships. What would your colleagues, spouse or friends describe you as?

You can then determine the steps you need to take to be more assertive and authentic in your relationships. What emotional blocks do you need to overcome within you? What inner resources do you need to tap into to be more assertive? How secure and confident do you need to be to engage with others?

If you tend to be more permissive, perhaps you need to overcome your fear of not being liked, or even being wrong? Do you need to build greater respect for yourself? Do you need to be more generous towards, and accepting of, your true feelings?

If you tend to be more aggressive, do you need to be more accepting of others and more empathetic to their situation? Do you need to be more patient? Do you need to tone down your dominating stance? Do you need to encourage others (particularly if they are more permissive) to express themselves more fully?

Sam is the regional managing director of a large technology business, with country heads of six offices reporting to him. He has been with the organisation for nearly two decades and has been highly successful in profitably growing the business across Asia. He is visionary, ambitious and a great conversationalist. He is also highly demanding and rarely minces words while letting his colleagues know of their shortfalls. The country heads respected and feared him—a pattern Sam believed was crucial in a successful 'boss–subordinate' relationship. However, in individual feedback sessions with me, the country heads expressed their displeasure with his critical and aggressive approach. They did not feel respected, and at times, felt humiliated in meetings. Also, they did not feel they had any sort of personal relationship with him after all these years, only a business one.

It took Sam a while to acknowledge the feedback and accept the need to explore other ways of being. What dramatically altered his motivation to change was his desire to fix his deteriorating relationship with his wife. Among other things, there were three insights that got him on the desired path. One, he saw an opportunity to work on his impatience. He recognised that he was always in a rush and invariably did not give his colleagues sufficient time to share their views. Second, he realised that he was susceptible to judging people based primarily on their IQ and achievements. In the process, he had lost connection with people and their emotions. He started to be more perceptive of how he was treating people and how they were experiencing him. These insights allowed him to be assertive while being patient, open and supportive in his interactions. Lastly, his big shift came when he began to question the merit of accomplishing business goals if people in his team did not feel valued and happy—an awareness that helped him start healing his relationship at home too.

Being assertive and authentic in all your interactions is crucial to building mature, open and meaningful relationships. This trait is pivotal to creating trust in your key relationships. It's an essential attribute of outstanding leaders. Besides, it would support you in feeling lighter, whole and enjoying a more fulfilling personal life.

Executive presence

An assertive and authentic communication style also feeds into raising your executive presence, a valuable leadership attribute. It directly impacts the quality of attention you and your ideas receive in a meeting. It also facilitates the building of initial rapport and relationships with others. Executive presence plays an important role in establishing your persona as a strong leader and shapes the kind of followership you establish.

Executive presence comprises four key traits. First, your *gravitas*—how well-poised you come across as in your interactions. Being assertive and thoughtful supports a sense of gravitas, as does being secure, self-confident and valuing your own perspectives in a healthy way. Second, your *credibility*—how reliable your opinions are. Being authentic, open and direct enhances your credibility and makes you more trustworthy. Third, the quality of your *communication*—how clear and inspiring your messages are. Again, an assertive and authentic style, coupled with relevant and meaningful ideas, increases the chances of you connecting with your audience and your message being heard. Being measured and succinct in your communication adds to your executive presence. Lastly, your *appearance*—how you dress and look. While many of us may wish this attribute was not significant, it does play an important role. Your appearance is not about being the best-dressed person in the room but supporting the right professional look for your role. Although your professional appearance is not a substitute for the quality of your ideas, it does add more weight to your presence and contributions.

Personal actions

1. Reflect on your dominant style, particularly in your key relationships. What would your team and other colleagues say your style is? In what situations and how frequently does it show up?

2. Among the leaders you have worked with over the years, who would be a role model in this area for you? What helps them be assertive and authentic? What difference does that make to their overall effectiveness?

3. What shifts would you like to make in this area? What needs to change for you to be more assertive and authentic? How would you know you are making progress?

4. How would you rate your executive presence? Which aspect of your presence would you like to focus on in order to enhance it?

Insight 6

From Being a Directive Captain
to Being an Empowering Coach

You cannot teach a man anything;
you can only help him find it within himself.
 – GALILEO GALILEI, Italian astronomer, physicist and philosopher

IRRESPECTIVE OF THE SIZE, LOCATION, INDUSTRY, FOR-PROFIT OR NOT-FOR-profit nature of the organisational context, a significant part of effective leadership revolves around managing and leading people. Leaders with high emotional intelligence tend to connect better with the people they work with. They can motivate each of their team members to be their best versions, thereby generating superior long-term results for the organisation. However, only a small fraction of leaders seem to get this right.

A leading indicator of this is the level of employee engagement in the workplace. According to the State of the Global Workplace survey conducted in over 150 countries in 2017 by Gallup, a leading global performance-management consulting company, the percentage of adults worldwide who work full time for an employer and are engaged at work is just 15 per cent. This implies that a vast majority of employees don't feel emotionally invested in their work. With all the supposed focus of organisations on their people over the last few decades, that's disturbing to know.

Employee engagement remains critical to an organisation for multiple reasons. As all leaders agree, people are an extremely valuable asset and a key source of competitive advantage. The higher their engagement, the stronger the advantage. An engaged workforce means lower employee turnover, higher productivity and better customer service. Engaged employees are more optimistic, solution-oriented and more willing to contribute to the team. All this translates to better business results. Gallup reports a 21 per cent higher profitability among the top quartile of engaged teams versus their peers in the bottom quartile. Simultaneously, it's expensive to have disengaged staff. They have higher absenteeism, lower productivity and create a lower morale in the team. Gallup also estimates that actively disengaged employees cost nearly $450 billion to $550 billion in lost productivity per year in the US alone.

What's even more important to note is that studies suggest that the quality of leadership directly impacts employee engagement. Gallup studies highlight that leaders account for at least 70 per cent of the variance in their team's employee engagement scores. That's a big deal!

What builds employee engagement? How do you inspire your team to fulfil their potential? HR and management consulting firm DDI defines employee engagement simply as 'the extent to which people *enjoy* and *believe* in what they do and feel *valued* doing it'. *Enjoyment* refers to the match people find between their skills and their job; it comes from a sense of autonomy and the opportunity to learn and grow. *Belief* refers to the confidence that what they are doing matters in the bigger picture of the team, organisation and society; and *valued* refers to the extent people believe the respect, rewards and recognition they receive are commensurate with their effort.

How engaged are your employees? How inspired are your team members? In this context, among the varying leadership styles, there are two that I would like to highlight.

If you are like most leaders, you were chosen for your position based on your high performance in previous roles and a perceived potential to lead a larger team, division or organisation. This is no different from being the captain of a sports team. Probably a star contributor as a player, a sports team captain simultaneously demonstrates some prowess to lead others. Like many successful captains, you perhaps lead from the front—focused as much on your personal contribution as that of your team, and are always willing to demonstrate how things can be done in a better way. You're likely passionately invested in the game and the results. Perhaps you like to delegate and divide goals fairly, into specific roles, among the team based on who is most suitable. You then direct the team in carrying out their roles, set up suitable mechanisms for rewarding and reprimanding good or poor performance and your team likely delivers good results. However, is your team at its inspired best?

As opposed to this more common captain-like style of leadership, is a coach-like style of leadership. Even with leaders from diverse backgrounds, I've often noticed a strong correlation between a coaching style of leadership and an increased level of employee engagement.

A coaching approach to leadership is rooted in three key principles. First, each of us has greater potential to learn and grow than is sometimes apparent. The answers to all our dilemmas and challenges do exist within ourselves; it's just that, often, with our busy lives, we are unable to devote the time required to seek those answers. A coaching leadership style focuses on tapping into that potential each person holds by helping to create the time and space for such self-discovery to happen.

Second, the most meaningful and sustainable change occurs when people discover solutions themselves. Neuroscience research demonstrates that the process of self-discovery creates brain patterns that are clearer and longer lasting than when individuals are told the answers by someone else. I am sure you have noticed how frustrating it can be to preach ideas to children, until they discover the lessons themselves. Besides, all adult learning theories suggest that adults need a flexible and self-directed learning approach.

The third principle of the coaching approach is that the best way to help others is through a conversation where we have no personal agenda or bias, we are non-judgmental and treat them as equals.

Together, these principles create a style of leadership that is engaging and empowering for team members. A coaching approach can effectively help colleagues learn and grow (through self-discovery rather than through direction); feel autonomous (from being self-directed, where they largely get to drive the agenda); feel valued (from being a conversation of equals, conducted in a non-judgmental manner); and feel empowered. Sounds like just what the doctor would prescribe for raising employee engagement and creating inspired teams!

Google conducted an extensive research in 2008, which was updated in 2018, under the name of Project Oxygen, among its managers and the wider employee base to determine what makes a good manager. The behaviour that came out on top as a determiner was 'the manager is a good coach'. Other traits that made the top five included, 'empowers the team and does not micromanage, creates an inclusive team environment showing concern for success and well-being, is productive and results-oriented, is a good communicator (listens well and shares information)'. Clearly, the coaching style works!

The question, then, is how do you embrace the coaching style of leadership? How do you bring it alive in your everyday leadership? Here are some ideas to make it happen.

Look for potential

There is nothing in a caterpillar that tells you it's going to be a butterfly.
— BUCKMINSTER FULLER, American author and futurist

Many a time, we judge others—a colleague who doesn't seem driven enough, a child who's not emotionally resilient or a life partner who doesn't express their love—and by that very act, view their traits to be permanent. Automatically, we become biased in how we interact with them. For example, we would respond very differently in identical circumstances to two individuals about whom we have different perceptions. If you have formed an opinion about a colleague being aggressive, you will likely temper your emails to him by either taming them down (to avoid confrontation) or using strong language (to pre-empt aggression). You would probably respond to a friendlier colleague differently.

Nothing inspires all of us more than knowing that someone deeply believes in us. Great leaders have a growth mindset—not only about their own skills and growth but also that of their colleagues'. As a coach-like leader, you operate with the belief that each individual wants to become better and has an inherent capacity for further development. What they need is a supportive environment to discover and fulfil that potential. When you believe in the other person's intrinsic motivation and ability to become better, you create conditions for real transformation. You then focus on their existing strengths and the resources that they need to tap into to make the required positive changes. You pay attention to where they get their energy from, the activities that make them come alive. You are also more empathetic to the challenges they face: Is the colleague really not driven or has he not found something inspiring enough yet? Is the team member not shining in the role or does the role not allow them to show case their skills? Is the child not resilient or have we been too protective?

Listen to understand

Good coaches are great listeners. If you want to help others discover their best selves, you have to listen to them carefully—not only to what they are saying, but also how they are saying it, and even what they are *not* saying. To inspire others, we first need to understand them. Instead of being directive, a coach-like leader is keen to listen to whatever a team member or a colleague has to offer. Such leaders listen with a genuine desire to understand what the other person is trying to say and where they're coming from.

Deep listening can help you learn more about people's inner thoughts, beliefs and motivators, which, in turn, can help you connect them to their own potential. Listening well is vital to building trust and loyalty. When you listen patiently, your colleagues feel valued and know that you care for them and their views. As poet Maya Angelou wrote, 'I've learned that people will forget what you said, people will forget what you did, but people will never forget how you made them feel.' How you listen to colleagues determines how they feel. It also supports them in feeling safe enough to honestly share and speak their mind. When team members are not scared to fully express themselves, it leads to richer solutions.

The majority of our conversations are directed by an agenda; whether the conversation is with our colleagues or our children, we want something done (ideally in our way). At least two-thirds of corporate conversations are 'push' conversations, where the leader is trying to push their agenda, often with limited regard for the colleague's situation or personal circumstances. An inspirational conversation requires you to be open to wholly engaging with another person, without knowing where the conversation will lead. Leaving your agenda at the door allows you to be totally present in the conversation.

How good a listener are you? As a start, consider observing yourself for a couple of weeks to determine your personal split between talking and listening in your typical one-on-one or team meetings. Any percentage less than fifty for listening is a sign that you have an opportunity to develop your listening skills. Seventy per cent or higher is a good score for a true coach-like leader. The higher the listening percentage, the more personalised and inspiring your solutions would be.

Ask, don't tell

When a leader engages her colleagues in a personalised conversation that's based on direct, open-ended questions, she's also having a direct impact on the team. Such conversations help team members become more self-aware, which, in turn, empowers them in their journey of self-discovery. Listening well and asking probing questions allows you to act as a mirror to your colleagues, helping them see situations more clearly. Besides, such conversations can support you in building a deeper understanding of individuals. This approach is equally relevant for resolving business challenges and any significant personal dilemmas.

I remember, during my corporate career, if a colleague walked into my office with an issue that was bothering them, my instinctive response would be to provide my perspective on the question—essentially, solve their problem. Why not? If I was senior to the person, I must be in that position because I knew more or had a better understanding of issues. While this might be a quick way to deal with the problem, and it might even be helpful in certain situations, it's not how a coach-like leader operates.

A coach-like leader meets the person where they are in their thinking and then helps them discover the answer themselves. They do so not by providing the answers, but by asking important questions. Coaching does not attempt to solve the problem, but shines light on the thinking that generated the problem in the first place. This empowers the individual to solve challenges on their own, given the right tools, in future.

A coach-like leader would ask a colleague facing an issue open-ended questions such as, 'What part of the issue is not clear to you?', 'How could you solve it?', 'What resources do you need to resolve this dilemma?', 'In what way can I help you?' and so forth. This is a very versatile approach. You can use it in one-on-one meetings, team meetings, appraisal discussions, issues related to interpersonal conflict or employee motivation, dealing with business challenges as well as to support your colleagues in resolving any personal dilemma that they may have. You may consider questions of this kind:

What conversation would you rather have right now?

How do you feel about your current performance?

What's coming in the way of your making greater impact?

What do you need to do to address that?

How else could you solve this problem?

What do you enjoy the most about work?

What makes that part so enjoyable for you?

What did you learn from this experience?

What would you do differently the next time?

What would you do in this situation if you were in my position?

What's the deeper purpose of your life?

What personal beliefs of yours might be coming in the way of your progress here?

What would you need to overcome within yourself so you can build a better relationship with this person?

How can I be most helpful to you?

These questions demonstrate a genuine desire to learn about your team members—to understand what's holding them back, their deeper motivators and their humanness. Such inquiries facilitate greater reflection on their part, a better connection with their inner self and a more open and engaging relationship with you, as a leader. Though such an approach generally takes a bit longer than merely providing an answer, it has two definite benefits. First, it forces us to arrive at the solution that's most effective in that team member's unique personal situation, rather than guessing at a generic formula or one that's worked for us in the past. Second, it helps that colleague learn how to solve such dilemmas in the future—*give a man a fish and you feed him for a day. Teach him how to fish and you help feed him for a lifetime.* The approach of asking, not telling is an empowering one.

Create autonomy with accountability

Just like the coach of a sports team, you must operate from the understanding that while you can *train* your team, you cannot *play* the game for them. Consequently, your focus should always be on helping your team members develop their capacity rather than on doing their job, even if you know you'd do it better. Besides, as in sports, as a coach, you must become comfortable not interfering with the team while they go about their business. This sense of distance allows you to create a much-needed space for your team members so they can explore, make mistakes, perform and learn in their own unique ways.

As a leader, then, you should neither overprotect your team nor nag them about their day-to-day outcomes. Many a time, leaders operate from the belief that active supervision is essential for quality results. This is a misplaced belief. It only disempowers the team and reduces engagement. Definitely go ahead and have quality feedback sessions with your team members to review their performance, but be very conscious to provide adequate autonomy for them to feel in control of their own destiny. This builds greater self-responsibility and ownership among the team members. Incidentally, a sense of autonomy is a key ingredient for creating a highly engaged team.

Sometimes, providing space for colleagues to perform can be misunderstood as an abdication of responsibility, where it's for the team members to sink or swim. Or, you may become hesitant to challenge them or hold them accountable, lest this should restrict their autonomy. This could lead to a laissez-faire situation, where every level of performance is acceptable.

Let me be clear here. Great coaches generate a strong sense of personal responsibility among their team members towards the agreed results. They are mindful of setting clear expectations with the team and getting their strong buy-in for the goals agreed upon. They're excellent at holding the team accountable, and they do it in an empowering way.

As such a leader, you would be neither too aggressive nor too permissive while reviewing performance. You'd be open, direct and assertive in your comments and feedback while simultaneously being supportive and ready to discuss ways that your team members believe could help them perform better.

Autonomy without accountability would lead to chaos, and accountability without autonomy is claustrophobic, stressful and disengaging for the team. Great leaders have a knack for finding the right balance.

Utilise the opportunity that performance reviews provide

Appraisals and performance reviews are precious opportunities to practise a coach-like leadership style. These discussions are invariably a tense time for both sides. The recipient is anxious about the feedback they are going to receive, and if it's appraisal time, then there's the additional concern about its potential impact on their rewards. It's not unusual for an employee to be defensive about any negative remarks they hear in such instances. At the same time, the leader providing the feedback is often uneasy about the best way to do so and the response their feedback might elicit. Directive leaders are accustomed to forming opinions about specific team members and sharing their views at such a discussion. This often ends up becoming a one-way feedback session with a small window for the recipient to respond. Even if the leader's views are founded in truth, the team members can walk away feeling judged, confused and powerless. In the process, a meaningful occasion to discuss performance and ongoing opportunities for development is often lost.

If you pursue a coaching style as a leader, you're more likely to actively engage team members in their performance review process. You will be inclined to ask them to prepare their own review of their performance, including their key accomplishments and target achievements as well as the opportunities they see for improvement. Your discussion would centre around inquiries that prompt reflection—things like what went well, what came in the way of better performance, what they feel they need to do better next year to be performing at an even higher level, what their career ambitions are, what they would like to be doing in one, three and five years from now, what skills would be required for those roles, which of those skills would they need to work on, what plan should they have in place so they progress on that path, in what way can you support their journey and so forth. Once you create a safe and a non-judgmental space for team members to be candid, they will most likely be more willing to be vulnerable, take greater personal responsibility for their development and thank you for any suggestions or guidance you may then add to their existing thought process.

Second, following a coaching style of leadership would encourage you to provide open, direct and specific feedback. Instead of either sugar-coating your comments—an approach preferred by many—or being harsh, you would be assertive in your communication. Most employees appreciate leaders who give them honest feedback, including on areas for improvement. The more specific you can be with your observations and suggestions, the better. Honest and specific feedback gives your team members a clearer picture to work with. In fact, it truly helps them grow. The best leaders do this in a supportive way that comes from a place of genuine desire to help their team members become the best they can be. When assertive feedback is provided with that intent and tone, it truly lands well.

Acknowledge actively

The last suggestion for embracing a coaching style is to acknowledge your colleagues more actively. I've worked with so many leaders who, on reflection, recognise that they just don't focus enough on acknowledging their team members' achievements. Somehow, they hesitate in doing so, as they view such achievements to be a part of the job. Some leaders also feel that appreciating their colleagues may make them complacent.

Surely, while any acknowledgement should be authentic, without which it loses its purpose, you can be generous with your acknowledgements. This is particularly true when you're coaching your colleagues on building new skills or personality traits—active acknowledgement serves as a positive reinforcement in their journey of change. Once you agree with them on the areas they need to work on, you want to encourage them for what's working well rather than be preoccupied with what's not. Everyone benefits from a little reassurance. It also strengthens people's self-confidence and inner security. As the German humanist and philosopher Johann Goethe noted, 'Treat people as they ought to be and help them become what they are capable of being.'

A truism I have noticed in organisations is that people don't leave organisations as much as they leave their bosses. As a leader, how you treat your team members has a profound impact on their relationship with their work and the organisation. Notwithstanding the pressures of your time or goals, when you focus on listening, being present for your colleagues without getting distracted by any personal agenda, being non-judgmental, empathetic, trusting and empowering, you inspire your team members to become the best they can be—and in the process, they fulfil their personal potential and contribute to the organisation immensely. While this may slow you down in the immediate term, it will prepare you and your team well for higher performance over a longer period.

Here's the little extra. Besides helping you be far more effective in your role, the coaching approach to leadership has some interesting side benefits as well. While stress comes with the territory of an executive role, it is believed that coaching others can not only reduce, but also reverse, the damaging effects of long-term executive stress. As Richard Boyatzis, a leading scientist in the area of the linkages between neuroscience and performance highlights, 'When they experience compassion through coaching others, it has psycho-physiological effects that restore the body's natural healing and growth processes, thus enhancing their sustainability. We thus suggest that to grow their effectiveness, leaders should imbibe coaching as a key part of their role and behavioural habits.'

Personal actions

1. Reflecting on the quality of listening, consider the percentage of time you're listening versus talking in meetings. What is your listening to talking ratio? What would you like it to be?

2. What personality traits would you need to build to incorporate the 'asking, not telling' approach? How can you empower your team more? How can you help them take more personal responsibility for their actions and development? How can you run performance reviews more effectively?

3. If there were three types of leaders—a cricket team captain (who is perhaps the best player and guides the team members on the field), a cricket team coach (who trains the team but is quite hands-off during the match) and a tennis coach (who is a mere spectator during the match), which one would describe as your current leadership style? Which other style would you like to add to your repertoire?

Insight 7

From Egoistic Confrontations to Breakthrough Connects

Nothing is a greater impediment to being on good terms with others,
than being ill at ease with yourself.

— HONORÉ DE BALZAC, French author and playwright

THE MOMENT THERE ARE TWO OR MORE PEOPLE INVOLVED IN ANY SITUATION, the risk of some form of interpersonal conflict arising increases. Each of us has a unique perspective of the world, and depending on how hardened that view is, we are not always willing to see it from another person's perspective. These differences routinely show up, both in the workplace and in our personal lives. When not handled effectively they can result in ongoing friction, mutual mistrust and a dysfunctional relationship.

Managing interpersonal differences is a vital factor in the quality of a leader's relationships across the spectrum—with seniors, peers, team members, clients and business associates. Leadership also has a lot to do with the leader's ability to influence others towards their point of view. Besides, they are often required to influence those over whom they don't have any direct authority—not only when trying to convince seniors and peers within the organisation, but also when managing external relationships with business partners, industry bodies and regulatory authorities. That makes learning to manage differences in opinions and perspectives even more important. When not addressed appropriately, these communication gaps undermine trust and pollute the work environment with negativity, resentment and a feeling of being wronged. This directly and adversely affects the morale in the workplace, the level of collaboration and, consequently, the achievement of goals.

Source of conflict

There are three key reasons conflicts arise among colleagues at the workplace. Firstly, due to our ego. With society's growing emphasis on individuality, we are becoming increasingly self-centred. In a competitive environment that offers disproportionate rewards for the successful few, our need to protect and promote ourselves can border desperation. We get attached to our point of view and its expected outcome. This attachment becomes particularly hardened if an alternate approach threatens our desired outcome. Coming from the belief that only one of the views can prevail, we see it as a win-lose situation. The ego, which manifests in the fear of losing and the fear of failure, something that successful people invariably hate to experience, makes it harder for leaders to let go of their point of view or to give in.

Leaders tend to evaluate every organisational discussion with such self-centredness, trying to gauge how the outcome would affect them or their team. In the process, the best ideas sometimes don't get enough support. This sense of insecurity also holds leaders back from generously accepting their own shortcomings or readily acknowledging any peers for their ideas or contributions.

The second reason conflicts arise is our judgmental nature. We idealise how our colleagues, team members and organisation should be. Anything different from the image we've built is a source of dissatisfaction. Moreover, with a fast-paced professional life, coupled with stiff targets, our tolerance for others takes a beating. We then harshly judge the other person for their differences. We feel at liberty to label them as selfish, inconsiderate, lazy, aggressive, overambitious, uninteresting, irresponsible and so forth. These labels prevent us from connecting with them more constructively. But as we cannot choose to avoid working with those colleagues, we are left to silently simmer, feeling frustrated and even angry.

Thirdly, conflict arises because of the limitations of our emotional intelligence—our inability to be self-aware and manage our own emotions and comprehend that of our colleagues. How well do you know yourself and your emotional triggers? What makes you frustrated, angry or envious? How skilled are you in reading your colleagues' feelings? Even if you are perceptive enough in picking up their emotions, what choices do you make while responding to them?

At times, because of a highly task-oriented attitude, leaders end up ignoring their colleagues' feelings, are quick to show their displeasure or even make highly discouraging remarks. If they lack emotional maturity, they take others' comments or behaviour personally, sometimes even holding a grudge against any person providing constructive feedback. This limited emotional intelligence is a serious challenge faced by some leaders in reconciling differences in their relationships, resulting in a continued festering of the interpersonal conflict.

Understanding the possibilities

Interpersonal differences do not have to necessarily result in dysfunctional relationships. Every conflict situation has several possible outcomes inherent in it, depending upon the way we show up in the interaction.

As an adaptation of the Thomas-Kilmann model for conflict resolution below depicts, there are five possible outcomes of a typical conflict situation. Two factors play a key role in determining the outcome we

Adaptation of the Thomas Kilmann Model

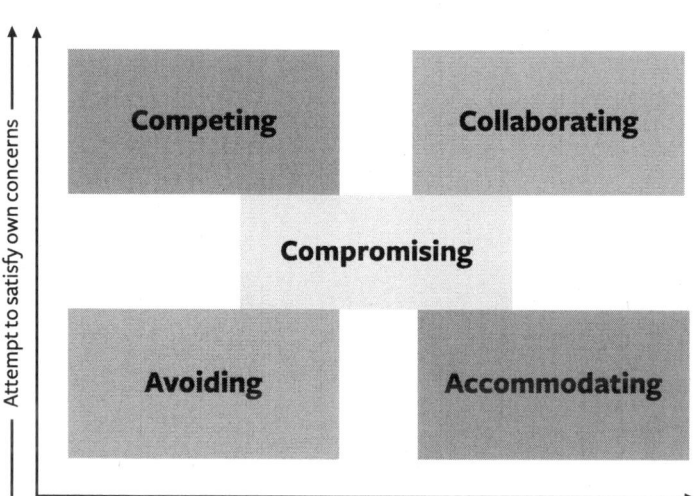

subconsciously strive for. The first is the extent to which we try to meet our own needs and the importance we lay on the achievement of our goals or completion of our tasks. The second factor is the extent to which we try to meet the needs of others and the importance we lay on the quality of our relationships.

I am sure you have seen all five of these scenarios played out in your workplace. There are leaders who see every disagreement as a competition that must be won—their agenda must be carried out. Then, there are others who are generally very willing to give in and accommodate to preserve the harmony in their relationships. Compromise is another popular outcome in organisational interactions, where there is some cooperation and some progress on the desired goals, although not nearly enough of either.

Though we do not always follow the same approach to a conflict situation, we do have a subconscious preference for one of these approaches. Unfortunately, other than 'collaborating', none of these common approaches are healthy.

The 'collaborating' approach is to leave our ego and insecurities aside and look for a win-win solution where not only are our needs met but others' are met too, where we not only progress on the agenda and goals but strengthen our relationships as well. Such an approach requires you to look within and examine what natural tendencies you have in such situations, and slowly create alternative habits and practices. Here are some ideas that maybe helpful to explore towards creating constructive connections in your professional and personal life.

From egoistic confrontations to constructive connects

1. Choosing to address it

All too often, leaders avoid directly addressing the proverbial elephant in the room. They are aware, and so is everyone else in the office, of the individuals they do not get along with and, for that matter, who among their team don't see eye to eye. However, they remain averse to uncomfortable conversations and wish the differences would somehow go away. Like a wound that festers, so do unresolved differences. Colleagues grow distant in their relationships, become uncooperative and, in extreme scenarios, may leave their job. Similar things happen in our personal relationships. The first step to managing underlying interpersonal friction is choosing to deal with it.

This requires making a mental commitment towards resolving differences and prioritising healthy resolutions over pandering to personal ego. You then need to set up some quality time with the concerned person to share your perspective and seek out a collaborative way forward. Likewise, you may like to bring together other individuals in your team who don't get along, with the stated agenda to help them find collaborative options.

2. Listening at levels two and three

Listening empathetically is pivotal to strengthening our relationships in general and to managing interpersonal conflicts in particular. Many of our differences arise because we don't spend enough time understanding each other's point of view. Not being heard upsets us more than not being agreed with.

As we discussed briefly in the last Insight, listening well means listening deeply, with a genuine curiosity to understand the other person. For this, we need to suspend our own agenda and be totally present for the other person. Listening fully also entails not interrupting when someone else is speaking, not finishing the other person's sentences, not reacting without thoughtful consideration to what is being said and not rushing to offer solutions before the problem has been clearly established.

There are actually *three levels of listening*. At level one, we are largely focused on our own agenda. We are constantly evaluating how what the other person is articulating fits into our game plan and impacts us. We are more focussed on how we are going to counter their argument than on understanding the other person's perspective. Concerned about how a colleague's comments might distract the team from our desired plan, we are very often listening at level one.

At level two, you are fully focused on the other. You listen to what your colleague is trying to say—not only their words but also the underlying emotions. The key piece of listening at this level, particularly relevant to confrontational conversations, is about being empathetic to the other person, their perspective and their context. Picking up the other person's emotional cues and acknowledging them can help build bridges in such conversations. One way to diffuse an emotionally charged situation is to acknowledge the other person for what they have said and instead of reacting to that, to label the emotions they are experiencing—*I heard you say you're often not consulted on these decisions, and I can understand you're feeling left out and frustrated about it.* (Instead of reacting, 'I don't agree with you.') This helps the other person become more aware of their own emotional state which, in turn, aids their calming down. More importantly, it makes them feel heard, understood and emotionally connected with you even if you do not fully agree with their view. Listening at level two can help build trust with your colleagues, and hence improve the chances of your ideas being heard and accepted.

At level three, you are not only focused on the other person, but also very aware of what's happening within you—the changes in your own body and emotions. Being fully attentive to the other, coupled with a highly self-aware state, creates conditions for engaging and helpful conversations. You are not only in sync with your colleague's mental and emotional wavelength, but are also very conscious of the mindset your responses are coming from. You are mindful of letting go of your own bias and choosing only those responses that will best serve your colleague and the agenda.

Listening at levels two and three supports us in actively relating with others. Level three, particularly, allows you to better influence others. When you are deeply connected with the other person in this way, unbiased by inner, self-centred thoughts, your ability to adapt your communication to what might be most useful to the interaction goes up. In that state, you are more focused on promoting what *is* right rather than about *being* right, about *working* on good ideas rather than *having* them and generously *acknowledging* other people's contributions rather than worrying about *getting* credit for yours. This way, you rise above the disagreements and naturally influence the direction of the discussions. That's what leads to powerful collaboration and co-creation of win-win solutions.

3. Responding instead of reacting

In an argumentative situation, we usually go into a reactionary mode. We easily become consumed by the emotions displayed by the other person—be it our colleague or our life partner. Their anger, fear, negativity or scepticism starts to dictate our behaviour. Guided by our ego and a need for self-preservation, we act with the aim to protect our turf. We react from a place of 'fight' or 'flight', thereby adding negative emotional fuel to the conversation.

Besides, our reactions are usually determined by our hardwired and judgmental perception of the other person. *He/she is always evasive or arrogant.* Consequently, we filter the other person's comments through this coloured lens, suspecting everything they say to be motivated by their evasiveness or arrogance. Clearly, that pushes us away from any chance of creating a win-win solution.

On the other hand, responding involves operating from a place of mindfulness—being fully aware of your personal emotional triggers as well as your preconceived notions about the other person. You then don't take things personally and choose not to get embroiled in the emotional drama of the other person. You are able to sensitively sift through the emotional noise surrounding the messages and respond to the real content. You also choose to be in a more neutral mental–emotional state, where you can objectively assess whatever is being presented on its own merits rather than be biased by your past perceptions of the individual and their motives. When we respond mindfully, we help resolve the conflict instead of aggravating it.

A simple principle that we are aware of but sometimes forget to put into practice: *try not to speak when you are upset.* We do a lot of damage to our relationships when we say hurtful things in anger during a heated exchange. It can take a long time and a lot of effort to mend the wedges created by these breaches. If you realise you are getting angry in an interaction, it may be wiser to ask for a timeout from the current discussion and suggest meeting at a later time.

Another situation where reacting instead of responding creates issues is when leaders admonish one of their team members in the presence of others. They may believe that shaming the person in front of the whole group will ensure greater collaboration (from the person and the group), they may want to assert their authority within the team or they might simply not be sensitive to the person's feelings. One golden role of creating trusting and respectful relationships is to *acknowledge people publicly and coach them privately*. Being criticised in public is hugely demotivating, whereas being coached about the issue in private is respectful, sensitive and supportive of positive change.

4. Being assertive and authentic

As we discussed in Insight 5, most of us have a predisposition towards either being aggressive or permissive in our interactions. These traits become particularly pronounced in an interpersonal conflict. Aggressive people believe it's always their right of way, are vocal about their views and are usually quick to display their displeasure in a disagreement. The permissive ones tend to reserve their perspective, over-prioritise harmony and are more willing to withdraw to avoid the risk of conflict.

When it comes to resolving conflicts, neither of these approaches results in the healthiest of outcomes—being assertive and authentic does. Let's assume you have a senior colleague who routinely expects you to work late or respond to emails over the weekend, and it negatively impacts your personal life and plans. A permissive approach would be to avoid any confrontation, believing that you cannot challenge a senior leader, and continue working late. An aggressive approach would be to walk out of the office when you need to or simply not respond to emails over the weekend. While it seems to suit your needs, it may leave a negative impression of you on your senior. A more assertive and authentic approach would be to set up time with your senior and have a candid conversation about how working late is significantly interfering with your personal life and how, despite choosing to leave a little earlier, you stand committed to meeting all your goals. It takes more courage to have a conversation like that, but it eventually serves everyone better.

In any confrontational and stressful group situation, the person who can stay calm, assertive and objective, and can articulate what is going on without a sense of complaint and blame, naturally emerges as the leader of the discussion. Such a leader is not only able to present their perspective more effectively, but is also able to pay attention to the concerns of other people. They recognise that not speaking up is not an option. Besides, they focus on sharing their perspective rather than worrying about whether their idea will win the argument or not. Being authentic in their commitment to finding the solution for the greater good of the group allows them to constructively influence others in the discussion.

5. Expressing your needs and emotions more appropriately

As an extension of the practice of being assertive and authentic in our closest relationships, we need to learn suitable approaches to express our deeper concerns and emotions more effectively. In valuable relationships, both at work and at home, we often experience sensitive situations where we feel at a loss as to what to say and how to say it. Even if we would like to be assertive, we are unsure how.

> Sumita, a client of mine, was routinely stifled by her boss' aggression but was at a loss about what to do about it. Another client, Jennifer, was deeply troubled by her uneasy relationship with her seventeen-year-old son, but struggled to get him to listen to her. While Sumita was given to sulking and feeling victimised by her situation, Jennifer was quick to get upset with her son's behaviour, and her interactions with him were often emotionally charged.

Here's a subtle but important point. When we are in conflict with another person, we usually focus on wishing the other person would somehow change their behaviour. But, there's always an unmet specific, personal need of ours that is the source of our inner conflict in the first place. This could be the need for respect, recognition, time, order, love, harmony, autonomy or something else. We are generally disconnected with this aspect within us.

> While Sumita wanted her boss to be less intimidating, what she actually needed was more space and autonomy. Jennifer wanted her son to listen to her, but essentially craved respect.

We can deal with such situations more effectively by learning to express ourselves in an appropriate way. Marshall Rosenberg, a well-known author and psychologist, elegantly describes this in his book, *Non-violent Communication*. He recommends taking greater responsibility for our own emotions and recognising that the feelings we experience are a direct result of how well our needs are being met or not. The approach, then, is to start by acknowledging, without any sense of blame or complain, which of our needs are not being met by the other person's behaviour and how we are feeling as a result. Once we have clarity on this, then we sensitively share it with the other person, without any insistence that they change their behaviour. He suggests expressing ourselves in the format of, 'When you do *x (arrive late to team meetings)*, I feel *y (offended)*, because my need for *z (discipline)* is not met.'

> Sumita and Jennifer applied this approach to great effect. Sumita gathered the courage to speak with her boss. After seeking permission to discuss something personal, she shared her need for autonomy and how, when he spoke in an aggressive tone, she felt offended. Jennifer found a tender moment with her son to mention that when he does not follow her simple instructions, she felt hurt and sad because her need for love and respect were not met.

This approach works for a couple of reasons. First, unlike our instinctive response to blame the other person, there is no judgment being passed on them or their behaviour. They don't feel blamed either. Second, we take ownership of our own feelings, by relating them to our personal needs. Finally, most people, when sensitised to the needs of those close to them, do make an effort to meet those needs. Ordinarily, we operate from the belief that it should be normal for the other person to understand our needs and emotions. However, each of us has a different perceptual lens, and unless we articulate our needs, others may not always realise they exist. Candid expression bridges that gap. As we practise this approach, we can not only have our needs better met, but also enjoy and nurture deeper, healthier and mature relationships.

Of course, this is not easy—it requires greater self-awareness of, higher sense of personal responsibility for and a high degree of willingness to be vulnerable and share our deeper emotions and needs. It also requires managing the impulse of judging and blaming another person.

Personal opportunity

Effectively managed conflicts can become a powerful learning experience. If you were to reflect, you would realise that what you don't approve of in others teaches you a lot about yourself. As we learn to listen deeply, choose to respond and not react, become more assertive and authentic in our interactions and more willing to be vulnerable and express our personal needs and emotions, we not only become better leaders but also grow as human beings. These experiences help us deepen our self-awareness and become more conscious of our own limiting outlook. They also encourage us to be more empathetic and compassionate towards the views of others. We need not relate to interpersonal conflicts as something to be won or avoided. When we have a healthy relationship towards such situations, they can support us in learning and growing from them and connecting with our own better selves.

Personal actions

1. Reflect on the people you tend to have disagreements with. How often does it happen? What are the recurring issues that are at the heart of these disagreements?
2. What changes could you make in your approach to arrive at a win-win solution for both sides? What opportunities do you see for listening better, being mindful in your responses, being more assertive and authentic in your communication and discussing your relevant unmet needs?
3. What difference would it make to you once these conflicts are resolved?

Insight 8

From Doubt and Insecurity
to Inner Strength and Confidence

People are like stained glass windows. They sparkle and shine when the sun is out, but their true beauty is revealed only if there is a light from within.

— ELISABETH KÜBLER-ROSS, Swiss-American psychiatrist

LEADERS ARE ROUTINELY TESTED ON THEIR WILL POWER, STRENGTH OF character and emotional resilience. Constant challenges, from experiencing setbacks to their well-formulated plans to full-blown crises related to their organisations, people or political and economic environments, are par for the course. Although some degree of self-doubt and insecurity at times of setbacks is natural, I have come to believe that its extent among leaders is underestimated. While presenting a brave face to the world, many leaders experience significant emotional turmoil within.

Do you ever experience the 'Imposter Syndrome'—the feeling that you're not as good a leader as people perceive you to be? Are you driven by a constant need to prove yourself? Are you easily affected by what others might think of you? Do you tend to be too hard on yourself? Do you tend to overanalyse difficult situations and take a while to recover? If so, I trust you'll find this chapter helpful.

Most of these feelings of inadequacy and insecurity are deep-rooted in our psyche. Some of us are born with a predisposition for having negative feelings about ourselves. Moreover, we acquire a large chunk of such feelings through our childhood and other life experiences. Being judged by friends at school, being neglected by teachers, not being considered good enough by our parents and underachieving on goals, all contribute. Such experiences negate our self-esteem and create self-doubt. When we don't value ourselves sufficiently, we feel a nagging sense of lack within. We then subconsciously turn to other ways to fill that void.

We seek external approval so we can be fully accepted and loved. We feel we are not loved or recognised enough, sometimes wondering if we are even worthy of love and acknowledgement. We hope for validation by pursuing success, money and status. While progress on this path can enhance our sense of self-worth, at least in the short-term, unless we strengthen our inner being and build our self-esteem, we will continue to experience a sense of inadequacy within, despite our outward success.

Another common way to cope with a lack of self-worth is to seek perfection in everything—it's our subliminal attempt at feeling complete in our own eyes and those of others. Yet, we are always short of our ideal, which we are constantly upgrading. Unsure of our own standing, we compare ourselves with others and are routinely disappointed as there's always someone richer, smarter, more successful or better looking than us making us feel worse about ourselves.

As we grow up, we continue to react to these emotional wounds of the past, particularly those that may have gotten reinforced over time. Unless we are able to acknowledge and consciously work towards healing them in our adult life, they continue to shape our emotional reactions and behaviour, directly influencing our effectiveness, the quality of our relationships and our resilience.

Insecurity and doubt get considerably accentuated in a high-pressure workplace. The perception of limited opportunities for career progression and the intense competition for them feeds our insecurities. Different leaders cope with these inner conflicts in different ways. To prove their worth, some plunge themselves into work and become workaholics; unable to let go of control, they micromanage their teams. To live upto their reputation as the most reliable leaders, others become perfectionists and lose the ability to prioritise. To protect themselves from the risk of not being liked, some adopt a permissive attitude and find it hard to hold others accountable; while some, fearing they will be taken lightly, turn more aggressive.

This directly interferes with our ability to lead others effectively. Nagging self-doubt makes us less assertive and more indecisive. Unpleasant situations make us fearful and even a small likelihood of any crisis is paralysing. Dealing with these inner upheavals consumes enormous emotional energy and leaves one with limited physical energy to effectively cope with the demands of a leadership role. These negative emotions manifest in stress, illness, burnout, inconsistent temperament, aggression and ineffective relationships. They directly affect our self-image and, in turn, our emotional resilience—the ability to bounce back from setbacks.

Great leaders fully realise that they need to build greater inner strength, deepen their sense of self-worth and enhance their self-belief. Here are four principles that successful leaders have found useful to build a stronger character and greater inner confidence during our coaching together.

Stop judging yourself

We frequently judge ourselves—our body, health, intellect, skills, relationships, likability, success and so forth. *I can never punch above my weight in a meeting; I am never the life of a party; I am not that talented; I am so weak at networking; I don't have it in me to be successful.* Such subconscious commentary is our perpetual companion.

To become comfortable being yourself, you have to accept yourself the way you are. Start with acknowledging your thoughts and feelings about what you don't like about yourself. Bring them out in the open and become aware of them. As they say in coaching, awareness is golden.

Gradually, start to accept those aspects that you are uncomfortable with—not from a sense of resignation but a genuine acceptance of the different facets of your whole being. Maybe you're not a great presenter. Perhaps you're not always comfortable speaking your mind. And that's okay. It's important to recognise that these traits don't make you a lesser person. If you'd like to build the missing traits, you can, but, again, not from a place of inadequacy, but because you choose to invest in developing yourself.

As Robert Holden, British psychologist and bestselling author, says, 'No amount of self-improvement can make up for any lack of self-acceptance.' Accept yourself fully for who you are and then determine the specific aspects you would like to work on.

Avoid comparison

Comparison is demeaning to our emotional self. Unfortunately, we routinely do it to ourselves and to our loved ones. The external world is competitive and draws us into a ruthless game of neverending, constant comparison—to most of us, it seems to be the only 'valid' way to assess our progress. Comparison, however, is only relevant when we lack clarity and the courage to blaze our own trail, the path that allows us to best express and channel our unique talents.

Each of us is unique in our own way. Celebrate your uniqueness and that of the others, without considering anyone to be superior or inferior. It's not always about becoming better than your peers, but becoming the best version of you that you can be.

There was once a monk called Soumya. While he was deeply committed to priesthood, he fell short of his own expectations and spent a large part of his life lamenting his lack of talent and his irreconcilable failure to be another Gautam Buddha. Then, one day, he had a spiritual encounter and a Spirit gave him some advice. 'In your spiritual after life,' the Spirit said, 'you will not be asked why you were not Buddha, but why you were not the Soumya you could have been.'

Let go of the need to be perfect

Instead of constantly seeking perfection in yourself, build appreciation for your own uniqueness. Move away from trying to perfect every little thing or win every small battle; identify your key values and the things that most matter to you in life and commit to nurturing them. Measure your progress around how well your life is aligned to those values.

Remember, you are wonderful and complete the way you are. Being wholesome and balanced in your approach is far healthier than constantly seeking perfection in everything. Such an approach increases your emotional strength. It also sets you on the path of growth and development with a sense of greater self-assuredness. As Brene Brown, the American scholar and author of *Daring Greatly*, reinforces, 'Only when we give ourselves permission to be imperfect, when we find self-worth despite our imperfections, when we build connection networks that affirm and value us as imperfect, we are much more capable of change.'

Be less self-critical

We routinely blame ourselves. We berate ourselves for lost opportunities, for making mistakes and for not being smart enough to avoid failures. We take every setback or negative experience personally. We then feel sorry for ourselves, which does no good to heal our emotional wounds of the past. Being critical of ourselves only reinforces our existing low self-esteem and insecurity.

Try not to be too hard on yourself. We all have limitations, we all make mistakes and we all experience setbacks. It's a part of being human, so don't take it personally. Be more compassionate and forgiving towards yourself. Rather than blame yourself, focus on what you need to learn and grow from that situation. As you operate from feeling secure within, you'll consider every setback as a valuable learning experience.

Padma is a senior marketing professional who leads the functions of one of the largest consumer product companies, and is highly regarded. She's passionate about her work and keeps long hours. She's equally committed to her family, tries to devote adequate time to her teenage daughter and keeps on top of running the household errands. When I first met Padma, her health had been suffering, and she just didn't seem happy. Discussing her stress levels, I once asked her if she really needed to be a 'superwoman'. Overcome with emotion, she broke down and mentioned that, for some reason, she always felt personally responsible for everything she was involved in. She frequently felt guilty for not being at home enough or not being her best at work. She'd always experienced herself as less than perfect and that bothered her a lot. Talking through this openly helped her recognise that, all this while, she had been too hard on herself. That, on balance, she was doing great on all fronts and trying to the best of her abilities. That she should be willing to give herself permission to experience joy and happiness in whatever role she is playing.

Positively affirm yourself

Reasons you are loveable

As Louise Hay suggested, 'You have been criticising yourself for years, and it hasn't worked. Try approving of yourself and see what happens.' She should know. Hay, well-known for her books on healing, rid herself of cervical cancer without any medical treatment. She got there by following, primarily, a regimen of forgiveness, affirmation, nutrition and therapy.

When working with leaders who are aiming to become more secure and confident, I often tell them to write down thirty reasons why they are loveable. Many of them are stumped by the exercise and struggle with the list—not because they don't have qualities that are loveable, but because they have never paid attention to them.

If you'd like to do this exercise, you can also seek the help of your spouse, children or close friends to build this list. You may be pleasantly surprised by the outcome. To affirm your inner self, remind yourself of the key items from this list regularly.

Reasons you are grateful

Likewise, I recommend writing down thirty reasons for you to be grateful in life. We often take positive experiences and what we have for granted. We're so focused on achieving, that we only tend to look at what's missing and what we are yet to accomplish. As you build your gratitude list, you will likely realise the special and unique talents you're gifted with. You may also better appreciate several other people who love you or have contributed to your progress—your family, teachers, friends, colleagues. At a deeper level, you will start to feel gratitude for the overall life you have, despite some of its imperfections.

Reminding yourself of these aspects will support you in feeling comforted, less anxious and more self-assured. Create a structure to remind yourself of the key elements of this list regularly. You can add two minutes of gratitude time to your daily prayer or meditation, or just practise gratitude first thing in the morning, last thing at night or while driving to work.

Practise positive affirmations

While we all, in theory, appreciate the benefits of being positive and building greater self-belief, putting it into practice is an uphill climb for some of us. Our instincts of feeling anxious, insecure or fearful are hardwired in our psyche and can be challenging to dislodge. Here's another exercise that can help you steadily establish new wiring.

Regularly writing or recalling positive statements about ourselves is a great reminder for our psyche that we are adequate, whole and loveable the way we are. This is a way to slowly displace the emotional baggage of our past. These affirmations reassure our 'inner child' that all's well. Repeatedly reminding ourselves of these affirmations slowly reprograms our subconscious to recognise its completeness.

Here are some positive affirmation statements:
- I'm complete, whole and enough the way I am.
- I love myself deeply and so does the universe and others around me.
- I have a wonderful life and I'm grateful for it.
- I'm thankful for all my experiences in life, as they help me learn and grow on my eternal journey.
- I see myself being successful, healthy and enjoying loving relationships.

You can alter these statements to suit your personal circumstances and include those that address your recurring negative emotions. Writing these at least a couple of times a day can be significantly helpful. If you can't get around to writing them, saying them aloud in your mind is okay too. However, you need to be mindful of three key considerations for this exercise to be effective.

First, I suggest you articulate all the affirmations as positive statements. The subconscious mind responds to the operating verb, action or emotion expressed in the statement, and aims to manifest it in our life. It does not judge between 'good' and 'bad', 'positive' and 'negative'. So, if you say,

'I am not angry', the subconscious will tend to manifest anger; whereas, if you say, 'I see myself calmer', the subconscious will be predisposed to manifest calmness. Recurring messages to the subconscious about abundance invites abundance in your life; fearing scarcity likely creates an ongoing situation of lack in your life.

Second, you need to practise these affirmations regularly for at least a few months. Creating new neural pathways requires consistent and sustained effort.

Last, you need to strongly believe in each of the affirmations as you write or mentally recall it. Being emotionally invested in these statements strengthens the potency of the messaging to the subconscious, and raises the likelihood of their being imbibed within your psyche.

Focus on intrinsic goals

Far too often, we are governed by externally visible goals. We chase a better job title, a bigger house and a fancier holiday destination. While achieving such goals is pleasurable and may also make us look good among our social network, sometimes it does little to warm the insides of our heart. Such goals, unless aligned to our deeper personal values, negate our true being and merely feed our insecurities.

Consider creating personal goals that are aligned to your true self—whether it's your choice of profession or life partner, your views on success or happiness or honouring your core values, not merely what's popular around you. Reflect deeply on what makes *you* happy. What nourishes your soul? Would you rather be a scientist or head a technology business? Just because heading such a business is more prestigious doesn't mean it will be more satisfying and meaningful to *you*. Honouring your intrinsic motivations strengthens your inner being and takes you away from social pressures.

Follow your purpose

One of the deepest and most intrinsic goals we can pursue is our own personal life purpose. Articulating and committing to this nourishes our soul, brings more meaning to our life and affirms our true self. We'll discuss how you can find your unique life purpose and more in Insights 12 and 13.

Build character

Conducting your work and life with integrity and honesty supports the goal of building a strong character. Even leaders with generally high levels of integrity sometimes choose convenience over doing the right thing. Remember, every transgression from the truth leaves a karmic impression of wrongdoing and guilt in our psyche, which, in turn, adds to our underlying insecurity. Choosing to do the right thing requires boldness, perseverance and self-control. Similarly, committing to living with our core personal values in all aspects of our life also builds character.

Why is character important? Higher self-worth and inner self-confidence come from investing in building a strong character. It also provides us the inner strength to keep forging ahead and the courage to see our failures as mere stepping stones in the quest for fulfilling larger goals. Strengthening the character nurtures the soul and creates a fertile ground for inner greatness to blossom; it makes us emotionally resilient. As Albert Einstein reminds us, 'Most people say that it is the intellect which makes a great scientist. They are wrong: it is character.'

Live a fuller life

Engage in things that you enjoy

If you're driven by an obsession to be perfect, you'll end up pursuing activities that you *should be pursuing* rather than the ones that you *want to.* From time to time, allow yourself to indulge in what you enjoy and acknowledge your inner needs. Valuing yourself in this way strengthens your self-acceptance.

Spend time in nature

Being in nature helps us connect with the rhythms of the universe and rejuvenate our body and mind. Nature's vastness takes us away from our limiting, insecure and self-centred mindset.

Invest in nurturing relationships

Invest time and energy in developing healthy relationships, particularly with like-minded people with whom you can be yourself and share your true thoughts and feelings. Such honest relationships can be therapeutic—the ability to fully be who you are and express yourself strengthens your self-confidence and helps you overcome any imagined insecurities. Besides, nurturing relationships are usually more supportive of your intrinsic motivations.

Help others

Helping others affirms our inner goodness, weakens the hold of our judgmental mind, lightens our burdens and makes us feel grateful. Seek opportunities to help others. Be kind to the people around you. Consider volunteering for a social cause that you care about.

Be open to seeking help

Always be willing to seek help from like-minded people who won't judge you. Such interactions allow you to be open and more comfortable in being vulnerable. Many a time, just sharing concerns and fears is enough for us to feel so much lighter. As we talk about our challenges, or their potential solutions, we clarify our own thoughts. If your concerns are deeper or you need more sustained support in this area, then you can also seek professional help.

Personal actions

1. Rate yourself on inner strength and emotional resilience on a scale of one to ten. What needs to shift for you in order to build greater inner strength, self-belief and resilience?
2. How often do you judge yourself, compare yourself with others or are self-critical? What would you like to change?
3. What are your key intrinsic goals? How well are you living and pursuing them? What would you do differently if you wanted to be driven primarily by these goals?
4. What else would you like to do to affirm yourself more actively? Consider making a list of thirty reasons you are a loveable person, thirty reasons you are grateful and four–six affirmations that you can practise regularly.
5. How fully are you living your life? What would you like to include in your life to live it more fully (such as engaging in things you enjoy, spending time in nature, helping others...)?

Applying the *Inside-Out* Approach: Mind

Insight 9

From Being Overwhelmed and Stressed to Experiencing Peace

Insanity is doing the same thing over and over again and expecting different results.

— ALBERT EINSTEIN, physicist

LONG-TERM STRESS, OFTENTIMES, ISN'T AN OUTCOME OF THE NUMEROUS problems we need to solve but, rather, a reflection of our attempts to solve them in the same ineffective way again and again. The sad part is that we become accustomed to such stress and even rationalise it as an inevitable part of a leadership role.

Not all stress is bad. Research suggests that some of it is actually good for us. Some degree of positive tension between our current state and our desired state propels us towards meaningful action. Positive stress improves our focus, raises our performance levels and supports us in achieving better results. It gets the adrenaline flowing and makes us excited. Life would be boring and stagnant without it. Some level of stress even grows our mental muscles and expands our brains. However, excessive or negative stress, arising from a sense of loss of control, can be debilitating. As wellness guru Donald Tubesing says, 'Stress is like spice—in the right proportion it enhances the flavour of a dish. Too little produces a bland, dull meal; too much may choke you.'

Excessive and prolonged stress directly affects your physical health. It suppresses the immune system, making you more susceptible to illness and infections; impacts your heart, raising the blood pressure and constricting the arteries; and leads to sleep disorders, which, in turn, have several negative consequences. Besides, stress results in reduced emotional control—you may become irritable, sceptical and disturbed—adversely affecting your judgment and relationships. You may experience lower energy levels that alter the quality of your presence with your colleagues or family. If not managed wisely, stress also hurts your cognitive abilities, slowing your memory and reducing your productivity and the quality of your decisions. This is because chronic stress can lead to the structural degeneration of the prefrontal cortex and the amygdala, the parts of the brain responsible for cognitive decision-making and processing emotions respectively. Chronic stress also alters hormonal levels and the brain chemistry. It leads to higher levels of cortisol, the stress hormone, and reduced levels of serotonin and dopamine, the neurotransmitters linked with regulation of emotions and mood. These changes are also linked with the onset of depression.

While we all recognise the negative fallouts of stress, the million-dollar question is how do we avoid it or manage it effectively? The answer to this lies in developing a better understanding of the sources of your personal stress and then determining the most suitable approach for yourself. Based on my observations, there are a few common sources of stress for leaders. Here are five antidotes, in response to those sources, which leaders find most helpful. While some of these may not be directly applicable in your personal context, I hope these ideas will at least provide you with sufficient stimulus to create your own plan to beat the burden of stress in your professional life.

Simplify your life

While the level of stress we experience is guided by a number of factors, including our emotional make-up and our mental outlook, one of the most significant sources of stress in our life is lack of time. We always seem to have more to do than we have time for.

Contemporary culture has led us to believe that we can have it all. Influenced by people's projected persona on television and social media, we seek perfect lives. We want to be employed in the fastest-growing professional field, be the most well read, be charming conversationalists, be super healthy, be with the perfect partner, have our children excel at school and outside, have an active social life and go on exciting holidays. In the process, we try to maximise our efforts in too many areas, fail to prioritise and end up with a never-ending to-do list. No wonder we are perpetually running against time and feel stressed.

One way to deal with that is to learn to simplify your life by actively making some hard choices. Here's a familiar story that makes the point.

A philosophy professor walks into class with a large mayonnaise jar and some pebbles, small rocks, water and sand. He challenges the students to take turns to come up to the front of the class and try and pack as many of the four elements in the jar as possible. The most popular approach students follow is to put the sand and water into the jar, and since all of that goes in, they are glad that at least 50 per cent of the elements are in. They then add the pebbles and most of those go in. For a lucky few students, one of the rocks goes in too.

Then the professor turns around and shows them another way. He starts with the three rocks on the table, all of which go into the jar. He then adds the pebbles, and there's enough space for them to go in as well. He then pours the sand and the water, and they seep through the little nooks and crevices.

The reason I bring up this story is because it's a great representation of how we live and work. We fail to identify what's important and prioritise it, and hence feel stressed about lack of time. We fill our days with sand and water—the stuff that doesn't add up to much. In the process, what get left out are the rocks—the things that matter the most to us. Reflect on three things that are most important to you in life, whether your health, wholistic well-being, family, relationships, helping others or professional growth. Then assess the extent of time and energy you are investing towards each of them and whether it's in line with what you would like it to be. Be sure to create non-negotiable time in your day to attend to these life priorities. Don't make your exercise plan or time with the family contingent on finishing work.

The same goes for your leadership. Today's workplaces thrive on constant action. If you are not careful, you can end up overcommitting time to routine activities and never have room for initiatives that allow you to make the greatest contribution and impact. As we discussed in Insight 4, stay focused on making progress on activities that are most important and strategic to your role. Set your priorities clearly, and take care of the rocks first. The rest is just sand.

I lead a simple life, a far cry from the typical 24/7 life of a leader of a modern organisation. While I am deeply passionate about my coaching practice, I restrict the time I spend on it to six hours a day. That gives me time to meditate, exercise or play a sport regularly. I cherish the meaningful time I have with family every day. Besides, I read a lot and spend some time writing. Not only am I now happier than before, I find my life more fulfilling too. One of the core reasons for that is that my days are built around satisfying my top three priorities—personal well-being and growth, family and helping others in their journey of personal and professional growth.

Likewise, within my coaching practice, I have chosen to be a solo-flyer and focus primarily on one-on-one coaching. In the process, I have let go of many opportunities to do group coaching work and partner with other coaches to create a larger and scalable coaching organisation. I have said no to multiple board and advisory positions, as despite being very rewarding in different ways, I don't see them align with my core purpose and priorities at this stage. Identifying your top priorities, where you add the greatest value as a leader, and sharpening your focus in this way will not only reduce your stress levels but also raise your effectiveness.

Let go of the obsession with outcomes

All successful leaders have a strong orientation towards achievement. They like setting audacious goals and going after them. That's how they become successful. The business world particularly thrives on such ambition. CEOs chase annual business targets and investors exert pressure on them by evaluating their quarterly performance on the basis of the stock price movements. Needless to say, targets serve an important objective—they set a clear direction to what the organisation is trying to achieve.

Being passionate about what you are pursuing is energising, but being overly attached to the outcomes is a key trigger for stress. The obsession with results takes your sights away from the process, and any risk to the achievement of your predetermined outcomes causes bouts of anxiety. Keeping your sight on goals is healthy, but getting attached to them is futile.

While you may have a great track record at achieving your organisational goals, it's worth recognising how little control we have on the most crucial outcomes of our life. Can you (as yet) control your genetic make-up? How about ageing and the degeneration of your physical body? How about death? What about control over the different organs of the body—how the heart beats, the lungs breathe and the intestine digests? We need to realise that in the bigger scheme of things, there's very little we can truly control in life. We can only be prudent in making the right choices in how we respond to evolving changes and manage our circumstances.

What is healthier is to stay focused on the process. Build a process, a methodology for your organisational goals, refine and update it as required from time to time and then learn to trust it. Be resolute in not getting too caught up in the short-term results and believe that the process will deliver the best results possible in the circumstances. Like the ancient scriptures recommend, your job is to focus on giving a 100 per cent to what you need to do, without being anxious about the results. This approach can release a lot of burden that you may otherwise be unnecessarily carrying on your shoulders.

Stop identifying with your work and title alone

As you spend more time at your professional pursuits, you begin to identify with your line of work or role or title. As the hours you engage with work grow, so does your emotional investment in it. When you're a star performer, this becomes even more pronounced. You begin to see yourself largely in terms of the work you do. You introduce yourself to others, and even think about your life, in those terms.

We just talked about the goal-orientation of successful leaders. The other related trait they possess is the keenness to *measure* outcomes. Measurement gives them a clearer sense of their progress—whether in office or on the golf course. Clear measures like salary, title, bonus or promotion make it easy to keep score of their professional life. Moreover, the progress on these measures is quite visible, even to others.

Unfortunately, there are no easy ways to keep score in your personal life. How much you love your family, how grounded your children are or how balanced your life is, are hard to measure and quantify objectively. Besides, it's tough to calibrate how well you are progressing in these areas. In a perverse way, this anomaly only serves to unconsciously draw you further to your work. The clearer and more visible the rewards of efforts at work, the more you get invested in it. Besides, the 24/7 nature of work, particularly with the likely global linkages of your leadership role, makes you stay connected with your work all the time. If you are not working, you are likely still thinking about work.

As you build such a strong identification with work, any ups and downs at the workplace have a direct impact on your emotional state. A confrontational meeting at work creates residual stress, a challenging email from a colleague late in the evening interferes with your sleep, falling behind targets makes you deeply anxious and any fear of being passed over for promotion or losing your job is paralysing. Given the importance some of us place on our profession, work-related stress often consumes us. Unable to isolate any unpleasant events at work, we let them pervade our life. We are preoccupied with worrisome thoughts, not only at the workplace, but also while having dinner with family or watching television.

To counter such extreme identification with work, consider reducing your work hours. Contrary to the correlation that driven leaders subconsciously tend to make between time at work and results, a study by John Pencavel, an economist at Stanford University, found that longer working hours have a negative impact on your performance. It suggested that productivity starts to decline after working fifty hours a week, falling substantially after fifty-five hours.

Simultaneously, you need to consciously invest in your other roles— as a parent, spouse, child, friend, community worker and responsible citizen. As you commit time and energy to these roles, your time and preoccupation with work is bound to reduce. Besides, as you make progress in becoming better at these roles, you will certainly feel happier and more fulfilled. In that state, you will naturally relate to your professional life for what it is—only one aspect of your existence. You will then be better-equipped to compartmentalise the ups and downs at work and not let them overflow into your personal life. Likewise, committing time to pursuing your personal interests adds to your sense of balance, enhances fun and builds a healthier perspective towards work.

Manage your self-centred orientation

Because of our self-centredness, we take everything personally. Our social bias, that worships 'winners' and ignores 'losers', accentuates this subconscious trait. We are quick to judge our successes and failures, progress and setbacks, compliments and critiques, and take them personally. We relate to slower professional success as a reflection of our inadequacy. Further, the belief that any single negative event may leave a black mark on our long-term prospects makes us deeply nervous. All this creates a lot of stress.

Happiness lies in appreciating that ups and downs are an integral part of human life and that it is futile to assume that one would experience only pleasant situations. Develop an understanding of the laws of nature and recognise that life is unfolding as it needs to and that every circumstance in our life is not necessarily a reflection of us. Also, no life circumstance ever happens uniquely to us—each one of us has our fair share of challenges; instead, it's how we react to them that makes the real difference. We don't need to take every person's behaviour towards us personally. Someone behaving rudely may not be directing it to you; it could well be that it's in their nature.

Further, no single event has as big an impact on us—positively or negatively—as it may seem to have at that time. Getting an early promotion won't change your life dramatically in the long term, nor will a promotion being delayed. It's merely our search for perfection in our lives that makes us exaggerate the importance of individual events. In addition, building a deeper sense of gratitude—which includes reflecting on and feeling more grateful for everything that's going well—is reassuring and calming. Such an approach provides a balanced perspective towards life, shifts our focus from perfectionism to wholesomeness and aids our experience of greater inner peace.

Cultivate healthy de-stressing habits

Some degree of negative stress is part and parcel of leadership roles. Yet, how you manage it can shape the extent of calmness and peace you experience. Here are some habits that can support you with inculcating inner peace.

Set boundaries to online activity

Let's be honest. If the first thing you do every morning is reach out for your smartphone, and the last thing you do before sleeping every night is check your emails, messages or Facebook, it's safe to say you are addicted to being online. Have you caught yourself reaching out for your smartphone every time you have a couple of minutes—while walking back to your office after a meeting, maybe while you wait for a cab or even an elevator, as you stand in a queue at a grocery store checkout or perhaps soon after finishing a meal with friends? This addiction creeps into our life and slowly enslaves us. Nassim Taleb, author of *Fooled by Randomness*, remarks, 'The difference between technology and slavery is that slaves are fully aware that they are not free.'

The constant mental buzz created by being switched on 24/7 leads to increased anxiety and emotional imbalance. Restlessness emanating from the desire to multitask and maximise our experiences is a significant source of increased stress. Excessive online activity interferes with sleep. This addictive behaviour often has the exact opposite effect to what we are hoping to accomplish through it; rather than improving our effectiveness and productivity, our performance suffers. We aim to maximise our productivity via multitasking, but end up having a fractured attention towards the task we were originally engaged in. Tell me if you can relate. While working on a presentation, you also keep checking your emails, cricket scores, Facebook updates, stock market moves and reply to a WhatsApp message. It's quite simple, really. When we're not fully present in the moment, our focus dilutes and our productivity deteriorates. Besides, our inability to be fully engaged in the moment seriously hampers the quality of our listening and our connection with people around us, including our colleagues and family members.

It is imperative that you create some clear offline time in your typical day—a non-negotiable window of time when you are not connected to any online device. It could be an hour or two every weekday evening or a stretch of time, say from 9.30 p.m. to 7.30 a.m., and a similar time window over weekends, say, Sundays 10 a.m. to 5 p.m. You can also choose certain daily activities where you must commit to being offline— be it at dinner, at the gym or while reading a book or the newspaper. Even if you are reading a book on your Kindle, you can choose to switch off the Wi-Fi connection.

Exercise regularly

Regular exercise is not only essential for a healthy body, but also for your emotional well-being. Any form of aerobic exercise is a natural de-stressor. Being actively engaged in something other than work, coupled with the physical action involved, relaxes the body and mind. It increases the production and release of serotonin, the feel-good hormone. This results in feeling more positive, confident and relaxed. Research shows that regular exercise can help in reducing symptoms of mild depression. Playing any form of sport engages your mind in the activity, helps you connect with other people and takes your mind off any stressful thoughts. Plus, exercise builds physical stamina and raises your energy levels, enhancing your capacity to deal with the physical demands of leadership. It supports better sleep which, in turn, helps your body feel better prepared to manage the daily ups and downs.

Get adequate sleep

Sleep deprivation is a serious issue for leaders. The sheer amount of work load and the accompanying stresses, odd hours of air travel, late evening business events and Zoom meetings, all contribute to inconsistent and poor sleep. The extent of sleep deprivation and its consequences are often underestimated by leaders. A recent Harvard Medical School study of senior leaders reported that 96 per cent of them experienced 'at least some degree of burnout'. One-third described their condition as 'extreme'. The point is, this state strongly affects any leader's attention span, judgement, decision-making, insight, patience levels, emotional intelligence and relationships. Stress and sleep deprivation form a vicious cycle: stress contributes to poor sleep and lack of sleep hinders our ability to manage stress.

Pay attention to getting adequate sleep. Jot down and practise healthy routines—sleep and wake up at the same hours; wind down the day with a book, perhaps some soothing music or family time; stop using your phone much before your sleep time; avoid caffeine intake, particularly at night, and *please*, avoid red-eye flights (trust me, you would be far more productive with saner travel hours!). Depending on your work environment, consider taking a power nap in the early afternoon—many companies like Google, Uber, Cisco and P&G offer sleep pods in some of their offices. For good reason; it's shown to enhance productivity.

Make time for meaningful and fun activities

Pursuing activities that you enjoy allows you to take a break and gives you mental relaxation. Besides diverting your attention from work, they tend to be fulfilling. Activities such as spending quality time with family, playing with children, meeting like-minded friends, walking your dog, pursuing a hobby, playing a sport, learning a new skill, engaging in something creative like photography or art, taking a vacation, travelling, reading or spending time in nature can immensely help you de-stress. They quieten your mental chatter and leave you feeling rejuvenated.

Practise meditation

The last piece of recommendation, and potentially the most precious, that I can share with you to help manage stress is meditation. Meditation is proven to reduce stress, alleviate anxiety, lower blood pressure and enhance serotonin production. Even a regular practice of twenty minutes a day can support you in feeling calmer, more self-assured, more focused, and instead of feeling stuck, more open to the promise of possibilities. It may be worth mentioning that elite performers in every field, from musicians, artists, media personalities, sportspersons to successful CEOs, have been progressively turning to meditation to manage stress, improve their focus and raise their game.

Personal actions

1. How would you describe your current stress levels—high, medium or low? How stress-prone are you? What are the most common issues or situations that you feel stressed about? Reflect on the impact your stress levels might be having on you.
2. Think of your ideal scenario in this area. What is different about you? What does being at peace look like for you? How are you responding to the same stressful situations differently? Which of your personality traits are strengthened for you to be in this position?
3. What specifically would you like to start working on now, towards manifesting this ideal scenario?

Insight 10

From Fixed Ideas to Reformed Beliefs

We don't see things as they are, we see them as we are.

— ANAIS NIN, French writer

WE ALL HAVE WHAT I CALL 'FIXED IDEAS'. FOR EXAMPLE, WE MAY HAVE FAIRLY rigid perceptions about what it takes to be successful, how children should be brought up or what's important in life. These perceptions allow us to effectively navigate our world and make the hundreds of choices we need to instinctively make to get through the day. These ideas comprise our perceptual map—the mental navigation system that guides us in assessing whether a colleague is trustworthy or not, whether we deserve to be angry about something or not, or whether it's better to speak up in a social situation or keep quiet.

The thing is, once our map seems to serve us well for the most part, we get attached to it and start believing it is the reality. We feel that we are good at understanding people and situations, and that what we perceive is the truth. We fail to recognise that this map is, at best, a *lens* through which we view the world—and there is a strong possibility that our lens is rather narrow and limited. While our judgement on the trustworthiness of a colleague may be right in many instances, it is not always right. When our perceptual map collides with a reality that's different from our perceptions, we feel conflicted, frustrated and unhappy.

In leadership situations, this limitation gets accentuated quickly. Since leaders are always in the spotlight, any gaps between their perceptions and reality are very noticeable to everyone around them. Besides, leaders are generally successful at what they do, which makes them feel even more strongly about their perceptual map. If they've been so successful, their perceptions and approaches must be foolproof, right? Not always. Again, while many of their judgments might be well-placed, they are not universally accurate.

In life, there often comes a point where your perceptual map is threatened with a force stronger than you may be comfortable with. It could be in the form of you facing a challenge in how to succeed in a new role, your spouse's beliefs challenging you more than before, your children disagreeing with your views more often, you feeling like you're failing at building a healthier relationship with your colleagues—you get the point. It's when your past approach somehow doesn't seem to work that you know it's time to review and refresh your perceptual mental map.

Beliefs: the core of your perceptual map

Our subconscious beliefs actively determine our behaviour. Behavioural patterns are nothing but a series of repeated actions, and how we act in a certain situation is based on how we feel in that moment—depending on whether we are angry, relaxed or anxious, how we respond to an email might change. Our feelings, in turn, emanate from thoughts. How we think about an issue determines our feelings towards it. If we think we have been treated unfairly by a business partner, we feel frustrated and angry. If we think winning a contract will get us closer to our next promotion, we feel excited and motivated. But where do thoughts come from? Now, here's the most important bit: all our thoughts originate from our deep-seated beliefs. What we strongly believe in shapes our thoughts and, in turn, our feelings, and thereby our actions and behaviour. Our beliefs also guide our perceptions and attitudes, shaping our entire perceptual map.

When you get upset with a colleague for not delivering results in line with agreed objectives, here are some of the underlying beliefs that might be at play for you: *everything must go as per plan; we must win and cannot afford to lose; showing anger would instil fear in my colleagues and ensure they never miss their target again.*

Likewise, if you are a workaholic, you may subconsciously believe that *success leads to happiness, everything must be done to perfection* or *pushing back on my senior's expectations would make me appear incompetent.*

Since beliefs are at the root of our perceptual map, any plan for creating a better-tuned map or affecting sustainable behavioural change must address the underlying limiting beliefs. It is important for you, as a leader, to recognise this. Every time you run into a conflict, in your mind or with someone you know, and every time you feel stressed about a situation, it's likely that some underlying beliefs are coming in the way of you developing a more positive outlook about that situation. As Anthony De Mello, spiritual teacher, psychotherapist and writer remarked, 'There is only one cause of unhappiness: the false beliefs you have in your head, beliefs so widespread, so commonly held, that it never occurs to you to question them.'

But wait, where do these long-held beliefs come from?

For us to appreciate our limiting beliefs, we need to understand how they get hardwired within us in the first place. That can help us in acknowledging their existence within our psyche and in working to reform them.

We acquire beliefs through various life experiences. To start with, as the ancient scriptures suggest, some of our beliefs are inborn. That's how two children of the same parents may display very different beliefs and attitudes right from early childhood. One child believes that work comes first, while for the other it's fun that should never be compromised; one operates from the belief that unless he's over-prepared he will underperform, while the other prefers to maximise output with minimal effort; one takes cheating lightly while playing a friendly board game, the other finds it appalling. Each of them is subconsciously acting from a certain set of innate beliefs about self, others and life.

At different life stages, the different key people in our life directly or indirectly influence our belief system. We form some of our most prominent beliefs during our childhood. One of our primal needs is the need to be loved. In our formative years, we routinely observe our parents, siblings and peers for clues to determine what gets us their love, attention and positive affirmation. Those clues form the basis of many of our deep-seated beliefs. Whatever attracts their love becomes hardwired in our psyche as a lifelong formula for being loved. If achieving top results in school or in extracurricular activities leads to acceptance and recognition from parents and others, we may grow up believing that winning is the most important thing in life. We then want to win at *everything*—whether it's an argument at work or a game of cards. We may start to judge others and ourselves from that lens. Similarly, if diligently following instructions from parents or teachers, without challenging them in any way, got us approval, we could grow up to become a conformist. We then believe that being conscientious and conforming to authority leads to progress. Alternately, if being aggressive, angry or a show-off helped us get noticed, we could subconsciously form strong beliefs around their merits. Likewise, if we rarely felt loved during those formative years, we could become withdrawn or reserved and believe that we are not loveable, no matter what we do.

Role models in society also influence our beliefs. Leaders in government, business and community as well as prominent stars in media, theatre, music and sports indirectly impact how we view the world and what we consider valuable. Many a time, role models guide our beliefs around success (think the *Forbes* list of the richest), fame (*Time* magazine's list of the most influential) and power. Observing their lives, we may also be more inclined to believe that success is everything and that it automatically leads to happiness.

Lastly, our beliefs can originate from our cultural setting. Our cultural and social background influence many of our beliefs, such as those about individuality versus community, career versus family and destiny versus free will.

The thing about beliefs is that they are neither necessarily objective nor can they be proven. They are just notions that we strongly believe in and somehow feel totally convinced about. Recognising how your upbringing and your environment influence your beliefs will help you shine a light on them so you can start to examine them in a healthy way.

What kind of beliefs are you living with? More specifically, how do they shape your leadership style? I, for example, have become aware of a few that have played a role in my professional life. I now recognise that my 'high performer' belief system resulted in me being a workaholic and a perfectionist. I tend to be an intense person, wanting to do whatever I do, well—whether work, parenting, planning a holiday or playing a sport. Another one: wanting to be well-liked, I used to have a tendency to be 'nice' to everyone. I would minimise confrontational situations with my colleagues and would sometimes avoid direct and honest, but difficult, conversations. Being 'diplomatic' comes naturally to me. I find it easy to empathetically connect with people, even those with opposing views, to arrive at some sort of common understanding. On the one hand, I can genuinely relate to each party's perspective, on the other, in this position (of the arbitrator), I don't feel pressured to take a stand or reveal my personal views. Over the years, as I have become more self-aware, I have been able to reform some of my beliefs, while others continue to be a work-in-progress.

Reforming our beliefs

Hopefully, you can appreciate the impact these deep-rooted beliefs have on your personality and behaviour and, in turn, on your leadership style. To refresh your leadership style and effectiveness, pay attention to these underlying beliefs. This will help you create a healthy mindset and progress on the journey of personal mastery and *Inside-Out* leadership. The good news is that irrespective of how we acquired these beliefs, we can reform them with conscious effort. Here is a five-step, simple yet powerful approach to make this happen:

1. Identify a leadership trait that's currently holding you back.
2. Articulate the underlying beliefs that may be at the source of this trait.
3. Explore some alternate beliefs that are potentially possible in this situation and create a list of all such beliefs.
4. Reflect on the validity of each of the alternate beliefs and shortlist the ones you consider as at least somewhat true.
5. Finalise the alternate beliefs that are relevant and would serve you well; start embracing them and find ways to stay connected with them.

Now let us apply this approach to some real-life situations. Let's say you tend to be uncomfortable holding your team accountable. All the same, you recognise that this prevents you from getting the best results from your team. It impacts the team morale, as the high performers feel demotivated when the underperformers are not pulled up. You've also received feedback on this from your seniors in the past. You have tried being 'tougher', but it feels very unnatural and forced. What can you do?

As a second step, let's consider the underlying beliefs that may be influencing your behaviour. Here are some likely ones:

• *I am dealing with responsible adults and it is improper to challenge them.*

- *Asking them tough questions would make them uncomfortable and may demotivate them.*
- *If I hold them accountable, they would feel I am a difficult manager; they would like me less and talk and think poorly of me.*

To create a list of alternate beliefs, consider this. Imagine you are in a college debate competition and the topic is 'Holding team members accountable is avoidable'. As you know, in these debates, one side has to speak *for* the motion and the other *against*. Assume someone just spoke *for* the motion and based their arguments on the above belief statements. It's your turn and you have to speak *against* the motion. What potential arguments can you think of to negate each of the above beliefs, even if you do not fully buy into those? Let's take a shot at this.

Belief 1:
I am dealing with responsible adults and it is improper to challenge them.
Alternate beliefs:
- Holding people accountable is an integral part of leadership.
- On occasion, we need to hold even responsible adults accountable.
- Holding people accountable does not in any way demean them.

Belief 2:
Asking them tough questions would make them uncomfortable.
Alternate beliefs:
- Although they may feel uncomfortable, being held accountable would make them more responsible.
- Asking them tough questions and building accountability is necessary to help them experience higher success and develop their future potential.

Belief 3:
If I hold them accountable, they would feel I am a difficult manager; they would like me less and talk and think poorly of me.

Alternate beliefs:

- I am responsible for being effective and not for winning a popularity contest.
- If I hold them accountable in an assertive and authentic manner, they would appreciate the feedback.
- They would like and respect me even more for being an effective leader (rather than perceive me as being weak).

At this stage, it's important that you maintain a non-judgmental state—that you don't judge yourself or any of your beliefs. Likewise, please don't judge the alternate beliefs either. The intention here is not to examine whether your current beliefs are right or wrong, but merely to expose yourself to the idea that there might be other beliefs in the same situation that might serve you better. As the fourth step, reflect on these alternate beliefs and objectively assess which of these might be true or at least partially valid in your case. You may find that most of them are true and relevant. Perhaps you can shortlist a few leading ideas from there. Say, you choose the following (please feel free to choose beliefs that resonate with you and serve you best):

- If I hold them accountable in an assertive and authentic manner, they would appreciate the feedback.
- They would like and respect me even more for being an effective leader (rather than perceive me as being weak).
- Asking them tough questions and building accountability is necessary to help them experience higher success and develop their future potential.

The last step is to bring these new beliefs into your conscious awareness and put them into regular practice. Be mindful of them during relevant opportunities, and consider some practical ways through which you can stay conscious of them. For example, remind yourself of your new beliefs before getting into every team review meeting. Initially, when you try to act on these beliefs, it may seem like an effort. As you do that enough number of times, they will start to become hardwired within you. As you practise embracing these new beliefs, be open to experimenting and then connecting with the changes they bring within you and to your relationships with your colleagues.

More examples

Like the previous example of a leader feeling uncomfortable when they're holding people accountable, there are numerous situations where a leader's limiting personality traits and behaviours can be reformed by examining the underlying beliefs. Here are a few examples of challenges that leaders commonly face. I have tried to highlight the specific challenge, the underlying beliefs driving current behaviour and a few corresponding alternate beliefs that could support behavioural shifts.

Challenge

Overly task-oriented and intellect-driven

Current underlying beliefs

- Focusing on tasks and goals is the key to achieving my objectives.
- With so much going on, I don't have time to focus on people and relationships.
- People value me for my intellect and ideas.

Alternate beliefs

- Focusing on the people in my team is crucial to achieving our objectives.

- If I could be more people-oriented and build engagement among my team towards our goals, I would not have so much going on personally.
- When it comes to the team, 'Nobody cares how much you know, till they know how much you care.'

Challenge

Overwhelmed with work

Current underlying beliefs

- Everything I work on must be of the highest quality.
- How can I say 'No' to clients or to other key stakeholders?
- Some of my direct reports are just not capable of delivering results to my expectations.

Alternate beliefs

- I need to learn to prioritise better; everything I work on doesn't need to be 'platinum' standard, some things can be 'gold', or even 'silver'.
- Saying 'No' to less important matters allows me to say a louder 'Yes' to what matters.
- With greater empowerment and one-on-one coaching, I can tap into the true potential of all my direct reports.

Challenge

A directive leadership style

Current underlying beliefs

- From experience, I know my solutions are the most effective.
- It takes too long to engage others to build consensus when I know what the most effective way is.

Alternate beliefs

- Everyone has great ideas, I just need to find a way to tap into their resources.
- My colleagues would have a much greater sense of ownership of this journey if they have greater participation or autonomy in decision-making.
- Engaging my colleagues in the process of decision-making, and coaching them along the way, would allow me to prepare them to take on more responsibility.

Challenge

Get angry easily

Current underlying beliefs

- Things need to go as per my plan.
- Others think they can take advantage of me.
- My anger would instil fear in the team so they will not repeat their mistakes.
- Not winning an argument means I am not smart enough.

Alternate beliefs

- The universe is evolving as it needs to, and it's futile to believe things will always go as per plan (remember sickness, weather and death).

- Other people's behaviour has nothing to do with me; it's the way they are. How people act is their karma, how I respond is mine.
- People get better motivated by assertive, empathetic and supportive leaders than they do by intimidating ones.
- I don't have to be right every time. I don't have to win every time.

Challenge

Too nice (feel helpless and like a victim)

Current underlying beliefs

- People take advantage of my being nice.
- I never get what I truly want.
- People don't fully recognise my contributions.

Alternate beliefs

- No one can take advantage of me, unless I let them.
- Maybe I am being too nice and need to let others know how I actually feel.
- If I let others know my needs well, they would support me in fulfilling them.
- Only when I respect myself and my time, will others do so too.

Challenge

Feel low from a setback (say, from being passed over for a promotion)

Current underlying beliefs

- This setback will affect my career.
- I will never be able to catch up with my colleagues.

- My life will never be the same again.

Alternate beliefs

- In the longer term, as long as I continue to have the right work ethic and continue to grow my skills, I will have a great career.
- No single event, pleasant or unpleasant, usually has the power to alter my life (or career) trajectory.
- This setback is going to make me more determined, resilient and stronger.
- Being passed over for a specific promotion does not make me a lesser professional or person.

Key takeaway

Every time you feel stressed, conflicted or stuck in any situation, consider applying this five-step process to assess your underlying beliefs and explore new beliefs that are more appropriate and will serve you better. Sometimes, you don't have to completely replace your current beliefs, but integrate the valid alternate ones into your existing belief system. You can also engage a colleague, friend or a family member to do this exercise with you. On occasion, you may be too set in your thinking, and involving another person in this exercise can help you bring in an independent, and perhaps a more objective, perspective to the reflection process.

It's easier to introduce new wiring into our psyche than to try to repair the existing hardwiring. Hence, it's more effective to focus on embracing and imbibing new beliefs rather than suppressing the old ones. Depending upon how deep-rooted the existing beliefs are, you may need to find ways to keep reminding yourself of the new ones. As you sustain this practice for various conflict situations, not only will those situations get resolved faster, but also over time, you would have refreshed and reformed your beliefs to reflect a more accurate life map.

Personal actions

1. List three of your greatest challenges at work, or outside, currently.
2. Follow the five-step process to examine your current beliefs related to each of these situations, the potential alternate beliefs and the relevant alternate beliefs that you would like to embrace.
3. What specifically can you start doing to actively practise the new beliefs? What resources within yourself will you tap into in order to make that happen?

Insight 11

From the Obsession of Doing to the Joy of Being

We don't attract in life what we want, but what we are.

— JAMES ALLEN, author

MODERN SOCIETY HAS A DEFINITE BIAS TOWARDS ACTION. THE NUMEROUS management practices structured around building a broad vision and then breaking it down to long-term objectives and short-term goals guide us in that direction. At a personal level, our obsession with individualism and the connected belief that we alone create our destiny based on our actions, pushes us towards a busier life. Besides, the constant reinforcement of attitudes such as 'more is better' and 'winner takes all' make us restless if we're without constant activity. We can't afford to miss out. No wonder, we live and die by our to-do checklists.

In Insight 10, we talked about how our beliefs shape our perception of reality and our behaviour. One of the most powerful subconscious beliefs, one that empowers our life, is pretty simple, really, and it is this: achieving certain goals in the future will, somehow, resolve most of my current challenges. It's an ingrained belief that only if certain outcomes were to turn out favourably, we would be in a much happier place. We live with this subliminal belief around the cycle of 'doing, having and being'. Here's how it operates.

We are possessed by the mental commentary that if I can somehow *do* this (get promoted, expand my business, lose weight, get my kids to a good college), I will *have* that (more money, more success, more time, more recognition, more friends) and then, I will *be* there (happy, fulfilled, complete, proud, grateful). While it is likely that there's some truth to this belief, especially in the short term, in the broader sense, it is illusory.

Because here's the thing, and I trust you can relate with it. When we finally *do* get promoted, we quickly realise that we do not necessarily have the extra time we had longed for or that sense of completeness we had conveniently assumed we'd be experiencing. Quite the opposite, now we need to prove ourselves worthy of the new role, and we are busier than ever before. Besides, no sooner do we start to get comfortable in the role, than we find ourselves setting our sight on yet another future goal—the next promotion. Now, as driven people and ambitious leaders, this is natural, isn't it? I'm not saying there's anything wrong with it. What *is* wrong, though, is when, in this process, we put our life on hold and postpone our happiness in the present by relying too much on the uncertain events of the future.

To transform our life and experience of leadership into a happier and more meaningful journey, we need to reform this belief. Instead of focusing on 'doing' and 'having' and considering the state of 'being' to be an outcome of that, start by choosing your preferred state of being and then letting that dictate your actions ('doing'). It is so much more fruitful to alter the sequence of this equation to 'being, doing and having'. Start by choosing the kind of person and leader you want to be, let that guide you on what you do and trust that with that, you will have all that you need.

Happy vice president or unhappy senior vice president?

Ask yourself whether you would like to be more successful or happier. If you had to make a choice at work, who would you rather be—a happy vice president or an unhappy senior vice president? I know what you are thinking, *'I would love to be a happy senior vice president.'* While being happy and getting promoted don't have to be mutually exclusive, forcing this choice is instructive. As you will see in Insight 12, success does not automatically lead to happiness. If you *had* to pick one of the two options, which one would you choose? Making this choice consciously can determine what you pay greater attention to, on a daily basis. That, in turn, dictates what you engage in, how you structure your life, what you have and how you feel.

While a majority of leaders tell me, although reluctantly, that they would prefer being a happy vice president (letting go of the idea of a higher position is *not* easy), they soon realise that their everyday actions are hardly aligned to that intent. They are usually relentless in chasing their career ambitions while often ignoring their inner emotional experiences. Just to be clear, if you wish to be the happy vice president, that doesn't mean you avoid being committed at work or stop being ambitious. You just become more conscious of your underlying emotional journey—how you are feeling from time to time as well as what makes you happy, and what does not.

Once you do decide to align your actions with this intent, a couple of noticeable shifts will happen. Firstly, you will start prioritising activities that provide you with deeper satisfaction rather than blindly pursuing activities that appear to offer a quick pathway to career enhancement. Maybe you love engaging with people and nurturing your team members' talents; perhaps you find fulfilment in driving special projects that explore and start new business lines; it could be you enjoy immersing yourself in creative activities related to designing new products or marketing campaigns. These may well be your best ways to contribute to the organisation's goals while experiencing a higher level of personal happiness and fulfilment.

Secondly, besides pursuing your professional goals, you would actively start to explore and invest in honing skills and pursuing activities that make you happy and nurture your inner well-being. This could be enjoying time with the family, exercising or meditating regularly, playing a sport or growing a creative interest. You would do this alongside your daily pursuits and not as something you wish to materialise as a reward for your future success 'some day'.

Plenty of research suggests that happier individuals make better leaders. Moreover, as you devote greater energy to activities that you enjoy, and are good at, your overall performance will likely go up too. Besides, engaging in meaningful activities outside the workplace make you a stronger and a well-rounded professional. As if in a mystical, odd way, although this was not your main driving motivation, you may well end up growing in your career much faster. You may start to lead a more balanced life, be less susceptible to burnout and have a successful career too.

Everyday leadership

Likewise, you can bring this approach of paying more attention to how you are *being* in the present moment to any leadership situation. Let me share an example. Every so often, I hear leaders lament at how overworked they are. Reflecting on what they need to change, one of the ideas they contemplate is being more strategic in their approach and focusing on fewer but meatier priorities. Curiously, they are then also quick to rationalise that this is just a 'passing phase' and that in a few months' time their life will be much more under control. They say they intend to start being more strategic after those few months. The underlying attitude is, 'Once I can get through this busy phase,

I can focus on being more strategic.' The reality is in today's volatile geopolitical and economic environment, coupled with the pressures of high competition, the busyness is unlikely to ever go away. If it's not ambitious organisational goals, it will be changes in government policies, increased turnover in the team or high market spends from a competitor. You will always have a good reason to be busy until you alter your approach. If only you could prioritise *being strategic now*, despite the seeming challenges, you will probably get through the busy phase more effectively. With this, you will have also further honed your ability to be strategic, which would serve you well in the future.

You can apply this approach to many other common leadership situations. Here are a few more examples.

Doing approach

We are currently pursuing multiple strategic priorities, and I personally need to stay closely involved with them. Once these initiatives are over, I will focus on delegating more to my team.

Being approach

If I can invest in being more empowering right now, it will not only help me accomplish these priorities more effectively, but also develop my team well.

Doing approach

I should attend more industry events to widen and grow my network.

Being approach

I should be more engaging whenever I get an opportunity to connect with someone. I should be more curious about other people, their ideas and interests. I should be more generous and be willing to help others succeed.

Doing approach
We must build a strong camaraderie in our team.

Being approach
Each of us must be authentic and supportive.

Doing approach
We must organise social events to motivate the team.

Being approach
I must be more inspiring as a leader. I must be more caring as a leader.

Doing approach
I need to build deeper relationships with my colleagues.

Being approach
I need to be a better listener. I need to be more encouraging.

Doing approach
Multitasking is the most effective way to accomplish big goals.

Being approach
Being present and mindful at all times is the most effective way to accomplish big goals.

Who do you want to be

With our achievement-focused orientation, we are obsessed with doing stuff. There's an underlying fear that unless we are engaged in *doing* something, we are wasting time and not working towards maximising our life experiences or fulfilling our potential. Even weekends and holidays are packed with activities, sometimes leaving us feeling even more tired at the end. Moreover, our preoccupation with doing is invariably linked with an attachment to some reward in the future, the idea that when we operate this way, we will gain success, recognition or happiness.

As against that, the *being* approach sets a direction for your work and life. Focusing on the state of your being is quite profound, because it gets to the heart of your existence—and, as a result, the person or the leader you want to be. It responds not to what you want to do or achieve, but who you want to be. Just for a couple of minutes, reflect on the kind of leader you want to be and contemplate the words that come to your mind. For example, you may aspire to be visionary, courageous, resilient, empowering, confident, strategic, authentic, generous, caring and so forth. How much effort and energy are you investing in being this way (as against chasing the monthly targets)? Once you consciously pay attention to developing these traits within you, it will directly impact the kind of leader you become. That, in turn, will help you bring your best self to the workplace and automatically raise your effectiveness.

Moreover, once you make the shift towards prioritising your inner state of being, it has a positive impact on every outer aspect of your life. For instance, you can apply the same principles to your personal life. Consider which words best describe the kind of person you want to be—loving, compassionate, mindful, calm, disciplined and so on. As we transfer awareness from *doing* to *being*, we shift from 'I need to control the kids now, and when they are more mature, I will be hands-off' to 'I need to learn to be more hands-off now (so the kids can become mature sooner)' and from 'Once I lose weight, I will love myself' to 'I need to learn to be more loving to myself (and I will be healthier)'.

Without the accompanying state of 'being', our doing is futile. If you are not loving to your family, spending any amount of time with your spouse or children will not be of great help. Unless you are authentic, however much you invest in your relationships, they will remain superficial. Unless you become secure and confident from within, no level of success will make you feel complete. Having said that, you need to discover your personal balance between the extent of focus on *doing* and *being*. The reason I am emphasising so much on the 'being' aspect is because a vast majority of leaders are already good and focused at 'doing', and it comes naturally to them.

Here's an exercise for you. Choose one or two items to focus on from time to time from your list of traits that describes the person or the leader you want to be. When you start your day, remind yourself of the person or the leader you want to be that day or that week. As you bring this into your conscious awareness, you might find yourself being more effective, productive, courageous, empowering or mindful—traits that would not only serve you as a leader but as a human being too. You could employ this plan before important meetings or during challenging situations. Ask yourself the question: Who do I need to be in this meeting (or this situation)? Do I need to be confident, calm, assertive or inclusive? Or do I need to be more open, empathetic, courageous or resilient? Being aware of your desired state would be of immense help in dealing with the challenge judiciously.

Have fun with *being* open to practising this!

Personal actions

1. How obsessed are you with *doing* stuff? Is your to-do list dictating your life and choice of actions?
2. If you had to choose between being a happy vice president and an unhappy senior vice-president, which one would you choose? Are your daily actions aligned to your conscious choice?
3. Reflect on the kind of leader or person you would like to be. What difference would you *being* this way make?
4. Which items of this list would you most like to work on? How could you go about practising *being* that way?

Applying the *Inside-Out* Approach: Soul

Insight 12

From Measuring Distance
to Pursuing Direction

We are not here merely to earn a living and to create value for our shareholders. We are here to enrich the world and make it a finer place to live. We will impoverish ourselves if we fail to do so.

— WOODROW WILSON, former US president

I WAS HAPPILY BUSY AT WORK.

Fortunate to have grown rapidly in my career at a relatively young age, I had become the CEO of Franklin Templeton India at the age of thirty-three. Our assets under management, one of the key yardsticks by which mutual fund businesses are usually measured, stood at US$180 million. I vividly remember the office party we had had previously to celebrate crossing the US$100 million mark. It had taken us three-and-a-half years in a challenging environment, since the inception of the India business, to hit this milestone. Franklin Templeton was known for its relatively low-risk approach to running its business. Despite that, my seniors had clearly taken a big risk in choosing me to lead the local business. I remember one of my senior leaders counselling me about my new role. I was told that given that we had already hit a high (in a challenging market environment), my top priority should be to manage any risk to the business and only then think about new growth.

In the following two-and-a-half years, supported by an outstanding team, we reached US$1.8 billion in assets under management. We had become a sizeable and highly recognised mutual fund brand in the country. We also received the CNBC award for the best mutual fund house of the year. I then heard that one of our competitors, Kothari-Pioneer, was interested in selling their business. Their international partner, Pioneer, had decided to exit India. The complementarity between their business and ours was striking and I could sense the significant gains from a potential merger right away. Gladly, my seniors were very willing to be convinced and we jumped in the fray. Long story short, we successfully acquired that business and that doubled our assets to US$3.6 billion. We went from US$180 million to US$3.6 billion in less than three years. Soon after, two months before my thirty-sixth birthday, I got promoted to run the Asia business.

The story of business success accompanied by my career growth continued. In the succeeding nearly four years, the firm's assets under management in the region grew four-fold. While work was terribly exciting, I was beginning to notice a couple of things about myself. Though I had everything going for me, something still seemed to be missing. This sense of incompleteness was hard to explain. I recall telling my wife about it and her being shocked to hear what I had to say. I had a great career, a loving family, lots of friends and all the material comforts. How could I *not* be the happiest person on the planet?

But I wasn't.

Besides, I was beginning to become aware of my own inner demons—insecurity, fear, envy and the need for external recognition were my frequent companions. As I looked around, I was unable to identify leaders who had successfully conquered their demons. If anything, the stakes seemed to only go up at the higher rungs of the ladder. I wondered if I had stopped growing as a person.

Coincidentally, around the same time, I got introduced to some

NGOs back in India in my personal capacity. Seeing these organisations actively bring about positive change was inspirational. It was oddly troubling too. It made me question my own life's path. I began to wonder: What difference was I really making in the high-flying job that I had? Did my existence matter in any way? Would I leave this world any better than what I had inherited? Simultaneously, I was drawn to reading a lot more—about the purpose of human life, the spiritual truth of our existence, psychological healing and social change.

Now, I am sure you are thinking, 'You were just going through your mid-life crisis.' Perhaps I was. I now realise that many of us ask similar questions at some point in our journey, but come the next morning, we get sucked into the routine influx of emails and conference calls— and that spark is gone. Luckily for me it just wouldn't go away. These thoughts preoccupied my mind.

Many years ago, I had learnt some meditation techniques that I found very effective both in my personal and professional life. But with busy corporate roles, they had become the remnants of my day—things you love to do but don't end up doing enough. Around that time, perhaps because I felt confused and conflicted, I had a strong desire to revive my practice. And revive it I did. Even though I was traveling frequently around the world, I found time to meditate every day.

Let's cut to the chase. What was becoming clear to me was that, despite all the adrenaline rush at work, being engaged in two things— my personal and spiritual growth and helping others, even though in a small way at that time—was giving me a very different kind of joy. This still small voice inside only grew louder each passing day. I knew I had to acknowledge it. I had an inescapable urge to create a life that revolved around these two themes of working on my personal and spiritual growth and helping others in some meaningful way.

My mind was buzzing with possibilities. I began toying with the prospect of starting an NGO, introducing wholistic leadership to organisations or setting up a social enterprise in the space of happiness and well-being. Somewhere in that exploration, I chanced upon the field of life coaching. It immediately piqued my interest and as I started to learn more about it, it truly captured my imagination. The connection was strong and a deeply intuitive one—it was a call from the heart. I knew I had found my calling. Luckily, I answered the call and my rational, left-brain did not come in the way. Coaching offered me a pathway to serve others—something that would add meaning to my life and complete what was missing for me. It also afforded me a platform to actively engage with my own journey of positive change.

As the idea crystallised in my head, I couldn't hold myself back. I didn't want to wait for a magical day in the future to make this change. The thought that a few more years in the type of role I was in would help me be financially secure wasn't as tempting. Neither did I feel the need to meet another coach (not that there were many in Asia then), nor did I analyse the economics of this idea. I was ready to take a leap of faith. It wasn't a career shift I was seeking, but a life shift—a life with the promise of greater happiness and deeper meaning.

The moment of truth arrived when I shared my plans with my wife. All through my soul-searching experience, I had been regularly discussing my thoughts with her. She's an artist. She is equally inclined to meditate and regularly volunteers at different NGOs. As she tells our friends today, I was so convinced about my decision, that she was very willing to support it.

That's when the journey began.

It's been over a decade and a half now and all I can say is that this experience has been a blessing. Professionally, what started as a vocation of helping others through coaching, has become a successful business practice. On a personal level, I have been disciplined about creating a life on my terms. The efforts I have been making in my journey of personal growth and change have been rewarding. I lead a much simpler life now, but it's one that I find greater happiness and meaning in.

Clarity of purpose

I have learnt several personal lessons over the course of my transition from corporate life to my present journey as a coach. One key lesson has been about discovering and articulating the purpose of your life—and then committing to living it. This idea of a clear purpose applies as much to you personally and as a leader, as to the organisation you serve.

One of the reasons organisations experience so much stress is that amidst the frantic pace of activity—from product launches to scrambling to meet monthly targets, from setting up new offices to frequent changes to the organisational structure—what's sorely missing is a sense of clarity and connection to a clear purpose. This is worth thinking about: What's the central reason for which your organisation exists in the first place? In what way does it solve the social problems of the time and strive to make this world a better place? How would society be worse off if the organisation ceased to exist? While most organisations line up their boardrooms with their mission and vision statements, how many have their everyday actions emanate from those?

Similarly, one of the reasons leadership has failed us in recent times is that it has become disconnected from a sense of purpose. This is also a key underlying cause for a leader's lack of fulfilment in their professional or personal life, despite all the apparent success. Consumed by a fast-paced life, we fail to reflect on and connect with our higher purpose. And what does all that manic busyness add up to? What's the point of it all? What makes your life worthwhile? If you believe in reincarnation, then what is it that you would deeply wish to pursue to make this specific lifetime count?

Perhaps such questions surfaced for you during the recent pandemic, particularly at the time of the complete lockdown. Undoubtedly, a time of crisis invites us to pause and reflect on what's really important in life. Besides, witnessing the sacrifices made by health workers, the plight of migrant workers and the personal losses of so many families, we cannot

not be touched by a powerful sense of compassion. It makes us grateful for our life and empathetic to the pain of others. Such feelings always exist within us but usually get buried in the busyness of life; we need to build on them and channelise the energy we have around them to shape our approach to life.

I ask these questions to nearly every leader I work with. After working with people for a long time, I am convinced that each one of us has unique gifts to offer and a special purpose to fulfil on this planet. But do we take out the time to discover what that could be for us at a personal level? We're running hard on a treadmill of activity, but often not getting anywhere meaningful.

As you relentlessly strive to climb the corporate, financial and social ladder, do you pause and wonder whether your ladder is leaning against the right wall in the first place? Which ladder do you even want to climb? Is it a true representation of who you are and what you want your life's work to be? What do you value the most? Do you want to be more successful or do you want to make a more significant contribution towards something meaningful? Do you want more money or greater happiness? Although they don't have to be mutually exclusive, which one is more important to you? Usually, we get easily consumed with measuring our progress with external and visible parameters of evaluation such as job titles, business revenues and the size of the cars we drive. I have a self-assessment happiness test on my website (www. rajivvij.com/happinesstest) that perhaps better captures our inner state. Hundreds of leaders have taken it, and I can tell you that the happiness scores of these successful people are rather scattered, a clear demonstration of a fact we intuitively know but often forget: success does not automatically lead to happiness.

Besides, we get stuck with the idea of relative success. We obsess not about how we're doing compared to where we started in life, but about how we fare when compared to our peers and our social network. The person driving a Mercedes C-class is constantly eyeing the E-class.

Meanwhile, the person in the E-class isn't any happier because they are wondering when they're going to buy an S-class. In the process, we, unfortunately, often live a poor life, because we are perpetually thinking about what we don't have rather than being grateful for all that we do. This leaves a vacuum in our life and we continue to feel not enough. Sorry to be the bearer of bad news, but unless your life is aligned to an overarching inner purpose, despite all the externally visible progress, you will continue to experience undercurrents of unhappiness and lack of fulfilment.

I urge you to think about that singular theme you want the rest of your life to be about —your overarching life mission above and beyond your everyday goals. Imagine you are eighty-five or older and looking back at your life: what pursuit would you be the happiest and proudest to have dedicated four or five decades of your life to?

Why it matters

> *The two most important days in life are the day you are born*
> *and the day you discover the reason why.*
>
> — MARK TWAIN, writer

Clarifying and living your purpose is liberating. It provides a direction to where you need to go, and can become the north star of your life's journey. Ordinarily, in our orientation towards achievement, we are driven by the idea of measuring distance—how much further we can go in our career; how much money we can make; how much recognition we can get and so forth. 'More' often means 'better', the underlying belief being that more success and more money equate to greater happiness. A pursuit of higher purpose changes that dynamic. It reconnects us to what's truly important and meaningful to us, to what nourishes our heart and nurtures our soul. Direction is more important than distance.

Let me share an analogy from the game of golf. As a recreational golfer, there's nothing more thrilling than hitting a ball really long. Unfortunately, in the pursuit of that rush, many of our shots end up in the sand, water or other hazards. With experience, you realise that getting a more satisfying score at the end of the round requires hitting the ball straighter, not further. Getting the direction right is more important than going for distance. A large part of our restlessness for 'more' emanates from the lack of a clear purpose in life. I would argue that finding your deeper purpose in life and climbing four rungs of *that* ladder is more fulfilling than climbing eight rungs of a ladder that's not an authentic representation of who you are.

A sense of purpose takes the place of an overarching life priority. It puts our everyday actions in better context, including highlighting the futility of many of them. Pursuit of purpose takes us to a higher ground, well above the mundane struggles of winning and losing. The patience and perseverance required to live a life of purpose builds character, which is a key element of the journey of personal mastery for our inner light to shine through.

Clarity of purpose also simplifies decision-making. In moments of a dilemma or inner conflict, whatever serves your purpose better is the path you want to take. Since our purpose is invariably aligned to our purest intentions, without the clutter of our overactive mind, the universe conspires to support us in moving forward. As we awaken from our spiritual amnesia and reconnect with the core purpose for which we were born, new people, ideas and circumstances present themselves in our life to propel us forward.

The most outstanding leaders not only have a strong sense of personal purpose, they choose to manifest it in their workplace as well. If helping others is a key theme for you, make it your mission to help your colleagues succeed—not as a means to an end, but as an end in itself. If overcoming your inner demons is what provides meaning to you in life, see the workplace as a great platform to practise being courageous, assertive, compassionate and mindful. This is what will make work fulfilling for you. As a leader, given the amount of time you spend on work, bringing your sense of purpose alive at work is crucial to your state of happiness and contentment.

Discovering your personal purpose

The talk around purpose sounds uplifting, but how do you find your true purpose? How do you know when you have discovered it? And does your purpose change through different stages of the life cycle?

Let me answer the last question first: no, your true purpose will stay with you for the rest of your life. Goals change, but purpose remains the same. When you figure out your true answer, you will know it within. It will be an aha moment and it will simultaneously feel so obvious. You will be able see that underneath all your deeper motivations, this is what your heart and soul have been yearning for, all this time.

Although, you do need to slow down and feel centred to reflect deeply on what matters most to you, there is no fixed formula to determining your personal purpose. Here's an exercise I generally have leaders work on: Complete the following statement in one sentence. *The purpose of the rest of my life is* _____. As you think about your key life goals, review what's central to those. Reflect on what will stay relevant for the rest of your life. As a leader, I am sure you are very used to planning for the next three to five years. However, this exercise requires you to think and commit to the next thirty to fifty years.

For example, let's say, nurturing your team (or your children) to fulfil their true potential seems like a super important life goal for you. What's the core theme for you here? Is it your team, children or nurturing? Which of these would be a lifetime mission for you? How would your life goal evolve if you stopped working, or after your children become adults? Maybe, the deeper purpose related to this theme is 'to help others succeed'. In which case, to serve that purpose, you could focus on your team or your children in the present and other relevant people in the future. Over time, you could help other teams in future organisations, people in your community, the underprivileged or social-sector organisations. Similarly, let's say, one of your personal goals is to be a calmer person or be less anxious. What underlying lifelong pursuits can you connect with here that you are motivated by? Is it to grow your emotional capacity or build inner strength or learn the skills to be happy?

Here are a few real-life examples of purpose statements of leaders I have worked with:

The purpose of the rest of my life is to...

— Be happy and make others around me happy.

— Liberate myself and others around me through exploration and teaching.

— Discover my best self and bring it to the world.

— Master my emotions, live by inner standards, help transform people and organisations and create happiness around me.

— Cultivate joy, love, purpose and courage for myself and make a difference to the lives of others.

— Use my talents and skills to add value to the world, my family and friends and enjoy the good things the world has to offer in a wholistic and sustainable manner.

— Be secure, assertive and impactful in my actions and give back to society by helping needy children get quality education, and thereby creating equal opportunity for all.

While each of the purpose statements is unique and personal to its author, I have noticed a few common characteristics among the more powerful ones. Firstly, they comprise two parts. One part is about the self and the other about going beyond the self. The latter part, about going beyond ourselves, whether it's unconditionally loving our children, making sacrifices for our family, helping the needy or doing something selfless for our colleagues, is what gives us a sense of meaning in life. That said, the first part, about serving yourself, is equally important. Because, unless you nourish and strengthen yourself regularly, your ability to help others is restricted. Unless you learn to swim, it's challenging to save others from drowning. Going beyond ourselves gives us meaning; that coupled with the self-work becomes a source of happiness for us.

Further, in my work with leaders, I've found that quality purpose statements are personal and self-directed. You can measure your progress on your purpose only by your inner standards. Your progress is not hostage to any external and visible criteria of assessment. Somehow, I have never had a leader talk about earning more money, growing in their career or gaining market share in their purpose statements. What's more, these statements tend to have absolute expressions of the individual's mission. They are devoid of a sense of comparison and relative achievement, things we otherwise obsess about in our daily life. While someone views pursuit of happiness as their purpose, no one says that the purpose of their life is to be happier than someone else.

Lastly, although leading a purposeful life goes beyond the seeming attractiveness of professional success, as I highlighted earlier, effective leaders are able to make the connection between their higher life purpose and their leadership, so they can live their life purpose at work every day. I am sure you can see how each of the above examples of purpose statements lends itself to the leader's professional pursuits. If a part of your life purpose is to make others around you happy, you can bring it to life at work by creating a happy work environment. Incidentally, happy leaders and happy teams are known to produce better results. If learning to be more secure, assertive and impactful is integral to your purpose, leadership roles offer numerous opportunities to practise that. Likewise, if the mission of your life is to discover your best self and bring it to the world, you can be mindful of relating to all leadership challenges as an opportunity to explore and discover your highest self and bring it to the workplace.

Personal actions

1. What's the purpose of the rest of your life? What is the overarching theme, pursuing which would make this lifetime meaningful for you?
2. How well are you living your life purpose in your personal life? What do you need to start doing to better live it?
3. How well are you living your life purpose in your professional activities? What do you need to start doing to better live it?

Insight 13

From Chasing a Career
to Following Your Calling

A musician must make music, an artist must paint, a poet must write, if he is to be ultimately at peace with himself. What a man can be, he must be.

— ABRAHAM MASLOW, psychologist

IN THE LAST INSIGHT, WE DISCUSSED THE IMPORTANCE OF CLARITY REGARDING our personal higher purpose. As you now know, while individual expressions of personal purpose are unique, the underlying pursuit almost always revolves around two key facets: one, working on our inner selves and evolving through a lifetime; and two, going beyond ourselves, helping others and contributing to making the world a better place. Moreover, this personal purpose is wholistic, and once we are committed to it, we can also live it in our professional life.

However, the most potent way to live your purpose professionally is when your work is truly aligned to your calling. Your work then is a true expression of your unique talents and delivers what you were meant to bring to this planet. It combines what you love doing and what serves society. If purpose sets the direction of your life, following your calling offers the vehicle to travel that pathway, particularly in your professional pursuits. When you are following your calling, work and life become less of an effort and more of a fulfilling journey!

When I discovered my purpose of continuing on the journey of personal and spiritual growth and helping others with theirs, I deliberated many ways to fulfil it in a professional or vocational sense. I thought of starting an NGO, introducing organisations to new and wholistic approaches to leadership or even starting a social enterprise in the wellness space. However, when I came across the field of personal coaching, my heart, mind and soul were intensely drawn towards it. I knew right away that this is what I wanted to be involved in for the rest of my life. As I rationalised later, I was so attracted to coaching because it allowed me to actively help others, stay connected with my inner journey and leverage my skills of listening, empathising and understanding a leader's mind. It has been my calling.

Relevance for leaders

The notion of finding your calling has implications for leaders in two ways.

As I highlighted earlier, if you are a leader, manifesting your purpose in your everyday work would greatly support your sense of meaningfulness and happiness. All the same, if you can pursue that purpose by engaging in your true calling, it would make the journey all the more powerful and rewarding. You would not only be more effective at your work, but also be a contented person. If you've already chosen to start a business, join the public service or serve in the social sector, because you knew deep down that this was how you could best bring your gifts to this world, then you belong to a small minority of leaders—the lucky few!

For the vast majority though, particularly in the business world, leadership is often an outcome of a successful career. You may have chosen a career based on whatever offered the best mix of growth prospects, financial rewards, status, security and challenge in the overall context of your skills. Arguably, given your managerial and other skills, it's likely that you would have been equally successful at many different career options. At the same time, we know that such success does not automatically lead to happiness, contentment and fulfilment. Perhaps these career options are, at best, a suboptimal combination of success and happiness for you. However, if you could discover your calling and make it a viable pursuit, you may discover your professional sweet spot, where the different dimensions of your professional life—success and happiness, progress and fulfilment, growth and contentment—are better balanced.

Secondly, people generally get into significant leadership positions in their forties and fifties. That's about the time they are beginning to question the meaning of life, their purpose on this planet and what they want the rest of their life to be about. After being in leadership roles for a while, many start to wonder what they want to do next. While some people are close to retirement, many are not. One of the burning questions for perhaps two-thirds of my personal clients who are in leadership roles is often *what next*? Some feel burnt out by their high-stress responsibilities, while others are keen to simply explore new and exciting avenues to employ their skills.

If you are experiencing such dilemmas, do engage with them—they can be the start of something wonderful in your life. If harnessed and channelised well, this restless energy can become a significant force for good. Instead of pursuing a similar role in another organisation or even succumbing to the peer pressure of becoming an entrepreneur in the same space, this may be the right time to listen to your heart and soul. The restlessness within may not be about a specific role or an organisation, but about the mismatch between what your heart wants and what your mind convinces you to pursue. This may be a good time to address that mismatch. In fact, I would urge you to actively pay attention to your inner voice and what it is trying to tell you. If successful professionals like you don't use this discontentment to jump start something meaningful—something that not only makes your heart sing, but also makes this world better—who would?

Jayant, an exceptional leader, had worked with a large chemicals company for over two decades. He had joined the organisation in the strategy team. Highly regarded for his business acumen, marketing knowledge and a wide network, he had grown to be the CEO of the business. At age fifty-four, and after twenty-two years with the organisation, he was in a dilemma—what next? Calling it his 'better half', he wanted to make the rest of his life count. After much reflection, connecting with his core values and needs, and clarifying his life purpose, he was clear that he wanted to commit a significant part of the rest of his life to helping the aged. He was drawn to the challenge of loneliness faced by senior citizens and decided to do something about it. He went on to start an NGO that supports the psychosocial and physical welfare of the aged.

Nilanjan is a dear friend. Loved by his colleagues for his intellect, authenticity and generosity, he is a wonderful human being. He reached the pinnacle of corporate success as the country head for a consumer products company in India. But something was amiss. Nilanjan was restless about creating a life that was fully aligned with his deepest values and that offered greater fulfilment. While he was uncertain about what this new life would look like, he was clear it was unlikely it would have anything to do with consumer products. His passion lay in teaching, harnessing the talent of promising managers and mentoring the youth. After much deliberation, he made a courageous move. He now runs a social enterprise dedicated to improving the quality of education for underprivileged children and youth. He has partnered with some technology experts to create a scalable platform that makes such education more affordable and accessible for all. The number of children the enterprise has reached and benefitted: ten million and counting.

Discovering your calling

The concept of a 'calling' is a rather intuitive idea—it's something so close to your heart that it's hard to merely *think* your way through it. In order to discover your calling, you must have as strong a connection with your emotions as you have with your rational thoughts; peeking into your soul might be more supportive of this discovery than leaning on your intellectual mind. Having had the privilege of witnessing the extraordinary journey of many individuals, I have created a seven-step process that can support you in exploring the idea of your calling.

1. Create moments to connect within

Slow down and connect with your inner being, your true self. To listen to your inner voice, you will need to eliminate the external noise. You need to get off the treadmill of unending activity and experience stillness. Unless you find these quiet moments of solitude, you are unlikely to chance upon your true calling. Enlightenment can be an accident, but you have to be accident-prone!

2. Visualise your dream life

From time to time, we all have fleeting ideas of how we would love our life to be. The idea of creating a vision is to be able to articulate and 'language' these ideas. Consider writing a note, describing in vivid detail, what you envision your dream life to be—not just professionally but as a whole. When you pursue your calling, there's a limited distinction between your work and personal life; both are an expression of who you truly are.

As you describe this vision, it's important that you are willing to let go of the sense of reality that often holds us back. This is the time to dream, to let your wishes be articulated. There will be enough time to do the reality checks later. Leave self-doubt and scepticism at the door. I recommend writing this note in the present tense, as if you were already living this vision. This lets you get a glimpse of what it would be like to live that life. Writing this vision statement will, hopefully, encourage you to introspect and explore what's truly important to you and what makes you happy in a more sustainable way.

Envisioning your dream life, think about your responses to the following questions:

What do you imagine a dream life to be? What life would you wish for, if there were no constraints, whatsoever? If you believe in any form of higher power and that power was willing to grant you the life you want, what would you ask for? What kind of work are you engaged in? What do you like most about it? What's your work environment like (size of the organisation, office- or home-based, in employment or self-employed)? What activities are you involved in outside of work? What does your 'ideal average day or week' look like? Where do you live? What's happening in your key relationships? What is different about you these days? What's changed within you? How're you feeling living this life?

3. Connect with what you really love doing

Besides building a picture of your dream life, you can explore aspects from your current life that can lead you towards realising your calling. The next three steps serve that objective. To start with, reflect on what is it that you truly love doing at work or outside. What do you relish and have the most fun being engaged in? Looking back at your life and career, what have been your most enjoyable moments and what made them so enjoyable? Do you notice any patterns emerging? Do you love working with innovative ideas, being creative, advising leaders of small and mid-size organisations, teaching, learning, being part of a high-energy team, being a catalyst of change or engaging with social issues?

Anthony served as the head of a leading real estate business. He loved the work but not necessarily the extreme pressure for meeting the monthly numbers. Describing his most enjoyable moments, he shared with me, 'Right from my college days, I loved the sense of autonomy and independence. Yet, I thrived on being a part of a community and building one. I didn't care who was driving and leading it, what mattered to me then was the sense of purpose. I recall building a community of football players. I don't think I was the captain, but I had great fun doing it. We had so many creative ideas and made several new connections.' He is now enjoying innovating and building a community of architects, interior designers and consumers.

4. Clarify what you are good at

Next, articulate your strengths—what you are truly good at. Based on the feedback you may have received from others, as well as from your own assessment, what are you most skilled at? Is it solving business problems, strategising, organisation building, bringing diverse stakeholders together, counselling colleagues, listening, being curious, empathising or planning?

Clarifying your strengths would be highly useful when you consider ways to pursue your calling. They provide you the capability to manifest your dream life and pursue what you deeply love doing.

5. Understand your core values and needs

Our core values and needs are central to who we are. However, in the busyness of life, including while running high-powered roles, it is possible to become disconnected from them. Maybe you deeply value empathy, balance or enlightenment, but over the years, you have lost touch with these values in your professional life. Perhaps you have a strong need for learning, creativity or growing self-awareness, and these needs are no longer being met in your life. If you are either unable to live your core values or meet your core needs, it is bound to affect your level of happiness and fulfilment.

As you explore the idea of your calling, make becoming aware of your core values and core needs an essential part of the process. True calling will allow you to fully live your core values and meet your core needs and knowing them is crucial for you to discover, and build conviction to pursue, your calling.

To get started, I suggest identifying five core values. Your values are principles that you deeply believe in and stand for—your personal code of conduct. Values are so important to us that we generally wish that others close to us, like our colleagues and family members, also follow them. Examples of values include impact, excellence, expertise, drive, integrity, humility, authenticity, loyalty, adaptability, resilience, nurture and empathy.

Likewise, identify your five core needs. Needs are the specific personal requirements that must get met for you to feel complete and content. Examples of personal needs could include respect, success, accomplishing, contributing, teaching, perfecting, love, friendship, security, autonomy, adventure and happiness.

If you need a reference list of values and needs to choose from, please feel free to visit my website at www.rajivvij.com/book/values-and-needs.

6. Serve your life purpose and a social need

We have discussed at length the idea of clarifying your life purpose in the last Insight. While connecting with your strengths, values and needs and what you love doing will offer you strong leads for discovering your calling, your purpose statement is a critical factor in clinching it.

A true calling invariably serves some contemporary social need as well. As we discussed earlier, a powerful purpose statement includes a segment that takes us beyond ourselves and towards helping others in some way. Explore how you can best live that part of your purpose in your professional life. What possible ways can you manifest it to serve others through your professional pursuits?

Here are some examples of professional pursuits that bring together the idea of living your purpose and contributing towards a social need:

— To invent apps that simplify people's lives.

— To coach people to be the best they can be.

— To create a social impact fund to help social enterprises thrive.

— To provide financial advice to help families become financially independent.

— To advise not-for-profit organisations on scaling up.

— To write and teach to inspire the youth.

7. Put it all together

As you explore the exercises from the above six steps, you will likely begin to get at least a glimpse, if not the full picture, of what your calling might look like. Such a calling is likely to be a true expression of you and bring together what you deeply believe in, what makes you come alive, your unique strengths and gifts, and the manner in which you wish to serve others. In Aristotle's words, 'Where your talents and the needs of the world cross, therein lies your vocation.'

Making your calling a viable pursuit

In my experience, two standout reasons that hold people back from committing to their calling are financial risk and social insecurity. If you are in a successful career in a stable, mainstream organisation, the risk of losing out on the existing trajectory of financial rewards can be quite worrisome. The reality of a house mortgage, children's college fees and inflation can appear daunting. The prospect of a tempered lifestyle and a smaller nest egg perhaps seem like imperfect outcomes. Moreover, you may feel anxious about a perceived drop in your social status. Professional success usually strengthens our identity with our work, and the thought of shaking that can be uncomfortable. Success can make you risk-averse.

Are these risks real though?

Thinking rationally, success should make you bolder. You are probably more financially secure than 90 per cent of the world's population. Having experienced success, you should be more confident than most others in succeeding in the pursuit of your calling. Having benefitted from professional growth, you should be more inclined than any other to give back and serve others. Society invariably respects those who have the courage to follow their hearts—because most people don't. The risk you face is not the potential loss of financial or social standing, it's the lost opportunity of nourishing your heart and soul and contributing towards a better world.

There are certainly some trade-offs, but as Nobel laureate André Gide remarked, 'Man cannot discover new oceans unless he has the courage to lose sight of the shore.' My work with clients in this space has shown me that if you are passionate about your calling and are skilful at it, it will eventually evolve into a viable profession. For me, personally, what started as a vocation, and a deep desire to help others through coaching, has become a successful business practice. As you embark on this journey, you should certainly be mindful of the need to acquire new skills and be willing to face some hardships along the way, just as you would in any new pursuit.

Alternately, if you are not ready to rock the boat or don't feel drawn to rethinking your entire existence, you may want to consider amplifying some elements of your calling in your existing professional world. Reflect on what is it that you deeply love about your work and how your work can directly serve others. Maybe it's being creative in solving consumer needs, being proactive in your research for new product ideas for a better society, developing people or driving socially relevant initiatives like improving diversity and inclusion or reducing organisational carbon footprint. Then explore how you can develop and grow those aspects of your profession in your everyday work. Ordinarily, while you're busy chasing organisational objectives, you can lose connection with aspects that are actually dear to you. Reflect on ways to stay connected with these elements and choose to be more intentional about them. Consciously expand on the aspects that are joyful to you and that serve others in your everyday work. This can support you in creating a new relationship with your professional pursuits and move you closer to the experience of following your calling.

Personal actions

1. Are you chasing a career or following your calling? Do you love what you do or do you love what your work brings (success, money, status)?
2. Follow the seven steps to discover your true calling. What difference would pursuing your true calling make to you?
3. If this is not the time for you to discover your calling (or if your work is not far from your calling), what steps can you take to make your day-to-day work get even closer to your calling? (Do this by amplifying the aspects of the work that are close to what you love doing, allow you to live your purpose and better meet your core values.)

Insight 14

From Programmed Reactions
to Mindful Responses

Between stimulus and response there is a space. In that space is our power to choose our response. In our response lies our growth and our freedom.
– VIKTOR FRANKL, Austrian psychiatrist and Holocaust survivor

EACH ONE OF US HAS A UNIQUE WIRING IN OUR BRAIN THAT GUIDES OUR responses to differing life situations. We are born with a karmic imprint of our predispositions and preferences. Our childhood and other significant life experiences build on that imprint. It's like we're programmed with software, and that produces a predetermined result for any situation we encounter. We thus react to a familiar trigger with a robotic predictability. Sure enough, our reaction invariably leads to the same result, too. Perhaps whenever you are stressed, you crave the same sugar-processed foods and eat unhealthy; every time your spouse is not ready on time for a party, you express similar frustration and have the same familiar argument; every time your child questions your perspective, you feel disrespected and respond in the same irritable way; every time you serve a double fault in a game of tennis, you feel awful and mess up the next few shots; every argument elicits a similar aggression in you and every setback revives an identical sense of self-doubt. Nothing changes. It's as if these instincts are predetermined. So much for free will!

In each of these situations, was there really a choice—an alternate way to be? Could you be more aware of your stress-induced craving and choose to be more watchful of what you eat? Could you be more empathetic towards your spouse? Could you choose to appreciate your child's perspective and engage with her in a mature way? Could you be more resilient and doubly inspired after every setback? There's always a choice. However, for us to not fall into the trap of our programmed reactions, and be in a position to make new choices, we need to be mindful.

Mindfulness

Mindfulness is the ability to be *fully aware* and *open* in the *present moment*. Being fully aware means being aware of what's happening within us and what's happening around us. It means being aware of what's happening within us not just at the physical but also at the emotional and mental level.

When you hear news of you not winning a coveted deal, what do you notice about the changes in your body? Do you feel differently in your gut, do your shoulders drop or does your back tense up? How do you feel emotionally—are you disappointed, frustrated, angry or anxious? What thoughts do you have in the first few moments—*this is going to mess up my budget for the year; in the race for promotion with this colleague this loss will show poorly on me; why do I always fail to close these important deals; if only the CFO had listened to me on the bid for the deal.* In a spiritual sense, how connected are you with your sense of life or professional purpose in those moments and how aware are you of your egoistic agenda? Do these thoughts, feelings and physical changes just happen automatically in the background or are you aware of them?

Mindfulness also requires being aware of your surroundings. This could take the form of being attuned to what's happening to people around you. What's changing in their body language? What thoughts are they expressing (or not expressing)? What's occurring for them emotionally? Like in a game of golf, mindfulness requires being aware of the unique conditions of your environment when you are about to strike the ball—the lie of the ball, the wetness of the fairway, wind direction and speed, hazards in the way of your shot and, most importantly, the distance between you and the players in front. It's also akin to an orchestra conductor being as aware of the overall symphony as of the individual instruments in the orchestra.

Besides being aware, you need to be fully open. This entails being open to all possibilities of the present moment. Ordinarily, we not only expect, but are attached to, specific outcomes in any situation. Let's say you are trying to counsel a team member and you want, and expect, him to agree with your views; if you have a difficult relationship with that colleague, perhaps you expect him to disagree. What you may not realise is how your expectation of the outcome and the relationship you have with the colleague shapes how you show up in that conversation. The way you present your ideas, the physical and emotional energy you display and how assertive, aggressive or defensive you appear, all reflect your state of mind. This introduces an unintended bias in how the conversation proceeds. If you expect resistance, you may become too pushy, and with that may encounter even greater resistance. Besides, if you're biased by your own agenda and expected outcome, you may be less inclined to listen fully to your colleague, and perhaps even become agitated.

Being mindful and open means that while you have a plan in place, you remain open to whatever may transpire in the situation. You are then better equipped to respond to what's occurring in the moment rather than being stuck with merely what you had expected to happen. You deal with the situation in a thoughtful and calm manner. You are more focused on arriving at a healthy outcome, rather than being attached to your predetermined one.

What makes mindfulness hard to practise

There are two key reasons we easily fall into the trap of our habitual patterns and programmed reactions. Firstly, our thoughts are predominantly related to the past or the future, rather than the present. Our mind, on average, has over 50,000 thoughts in a given day. Even while you're busy with a certain task, the mind is forever racing ahead with numerous other thoughts—of potential risks and rewards, missed opportunities, relationships, commitments and so on. This mental chatter is no passing cloud, but a permanent 'noise' in the background. While some of this noise propels us to take meaningful action towards our goals, much of it is dysfunctional. It restricts us from being fully in the present, resulting in lower effectiveness and a diluted sense of fulfilment. Besides, all these thoughts are accompanied by corresponding emotions which fill our being and interfere with our emotional equilibrium, making us restless, confused and impulsive.

Secondly, over the last two decades, our attention span has shrunk dramatically. The overload of stimuli—instant messaging that encourages split-second responses, social media and clickable access to an unimaginable wealth of information—makes it harder to focus on any one thing fully. Two-minute videos are way more popular than thoughtful talks of thirty minutes. Most people don't have the patience or the attention span to sit through longer talks, articles or books anymore. You barely read a page of a book before you are tempted to check your email. In the meantime, you get two new WhatsApp messages, and before you are done responding to them, you remember you wanted to look up the new restaurant that you heard about at lunch earlier in the day. The search reveals two other restaurants that look rather interesting, and you explore more. Too bad you didn't have any time for the book!

Moreover, as we reflected on earlier, multitasking is revered in the workplace. This makes you susceptible to biting off more than you can chew. Overwhelmed with the amount that is going on, your ability to be aware of yourself and your surroundings and stay open to all the possibilities of the moment gets numbed. The never-ending temptation to juggle multiple priorities means divided and incomplete attention to individual priorities. You find yourself wanting to read while running on the treadmill, answer emails while in the loo and text at the dinner table. It's a struggle being mindful that way.

Underneath a lot of these tendencies is our insecurity around missing out. We want it all and are unwilling to prioritise and make choices. The desire for a perfect life keeps our mind steadfastly trained on thoughts about the uncertainty of future outcomes and missed opportunities of the past. Ironically, only when we learn to be more mindful, can we become better-equipped to connect with our calmer inner self and slowly work through these insecurities.

Relevance for leaders

Learning the skills to be mindful is crucial for sustaining effective leadership. Leading from a place of deeper awareness and greater openness has wide-ranging positive implications for you and your organisation. Likewise, a lack of mindfulness has a direct negative impact on the quality of your leadership. Multitasking and feeling rushed eventually dull your ability to make judicious choices and be creative. Researchers at the Institute of Psychiatry at the University of London studied 1,100 workers at a British company, and found that, over time, multitasking with electronic media caused a greater decrease in IQ than smoking pot or losing a night's sleep.

Being a mindful leader also helps you eliminate your cognitive biases. A cognitive bias, sometimes linked to a limiting belief, is the tendency to make erroneous decisions and judgments based on a fixed way of looking at a problem, whether on the basis of your past experiences, emotional make-up or self-interest. For example, many of us have confirmation bias, whereby we focus only on the data that confirms our viewpoint. In an organisational context, cognitive biases include a tendency to throw resources at a problem (illusion of control bias), overemphasise risk-taking, creativity and innovation (anti-status quo bias) and excessively focus on action over planning (reaction-time bias). Perth Leadership Institute's research has established how such biases significantly impact the financial results of an organisation. However, when you are more mindful, you can more clearly identify these biases and may be willing to consider alternate choices.

Leadership invariably includes dealing with unpredictable events and crisis situations. Being mindful supports you in maintaining a better emotional and mental equilibrium in the face of such challenges. You are then better positioned to assess the objective reality of the situation and isolate the noise emanating from your own or another person's emotional state. If you are unable to connect with your own fear and anxiety, the threat of the event likely appears much larger than it is. When you are more open to all possibilities of the present moment, you have a greater acceptance of the current reality. You then spend less energy on blaming yourself or others and are more focused on what needs to be done in the present to move forward. You are able to switch off the anxious thoughts of 'what could have been' or 'what might turn out to be' and, instead, engage in the present moment to the best of your abilities.

Imagine how wasteful it would have been for Roger Federer, down at 1-4 in the final set of the 2017 Australian Open against Rafael Nadal, to regret how he lost his last serve or worry about what this might mean for his chances of winning the championship. What he needed at that stage was to stay focused on the current game and play each point to the best of his ability. And that required being mindful, being *totally* immersed in the present moment. That's what he did incredibly well, eventually winning the set 6-4, and thereby the championship.

As a leader, being mindful can dramatically alter your professional as well as personal relationships. Mindfulness enhances your listening ability. You are able to connect with not only what is being said, but also what is not. You are better attuned to the emotional state of the other person and are more empathetic. You can better acknowledge the other person. Being fully open, you are willing to let go of your personal agenda and are more focused on making it a meaningful and productive conversation. All of these outcomes enable deeper relationships. One of the top leadership traits that employees attribute their motivation levels to, is the leader's empathetic and caring attitude. Mindfulness strengthens that.

The idea of mindfulness is directly linked with being fully engaged in the moment. It is akin to the notion of 'flow', coined by Hungarian psychologist Mihaly Csikszentmihalyi. 'Flow' is described as a mental state of being fully immersed in the task at hand, so much so that you completely lose sense of time and space. Our general attention deficit and preference for multitasking makes our engagement with any task or person shallow. We work really hard but don't feel satisfied. A state of flow, where we are engaged deeply with whatever we are involved in, is essential to experiencing deeper happiness and a sense of fulfilment. It can be a highly nourishing and motivating force within.

Lastly, mindfulness helps you feel calmer and more at peace. As a leader, it equips you to neutralise your anxious and addictive behaviours—addiction to email, preoccupation with thoughts of work commitments and restlessness about the future. Being mindful of your thoughts and actions encourages you to pause and make effective choices: choices about how much time to devote to emails, how much to let go of work-related thoughts, how much to relax and engage in activities outside of work and so on. Mindfulness enhances impulse control, which, in turn, builds character, adds fulfilment and improves happiness. It can also support you in being less of a perfectionist and learning to be at peace with where things are without anxiously trying to get where you would like them to be. Being mindful reduces your anxiety levels and heart rate, which are important for both physical health as well as overall well-being.

Cultivating mindfulness

We all recognise that the mind is the key to our success and happiness. Your attitudes, perceptions, beliefs and outlook directly affect your experiences as a leader at work, or in your relationships, and your emotional well-being. But how much time and energy do you invest in nurturing your mental well-being and growth? Cultivating mindfulness is central to this practice. Any amount of time and energy invested in developing mindfulness will offer you enormous returns; it may well be one of your best investments ever. Just to reiterate, mindfulness consists of two key tenets: being fully aware in the present and staying open to all possibilities. Here are four ideas to support you in developing the skills for mindfulness.

1. Focusing on the present

As against the temptation of multitasking, choose to focus on one thing at a time. If you are in a meeting, switch off your phone and be fully engaged in the meeting; when preparing for an important presentation, avoid checking your emails and text messages. A couple of habits can help you build this discipline. Firstly, create specific time windows in the day to respond to emails. This helps keep your mind from being constantly distracted by new messages popping up in your inbox or by the thoughts of your expected responses. Though checking and responding to emails offers instant gratification, it detracts you from engaging in more strategic and meaningful agenda. While writing this book on my laptop, there were many times when I switched off its Wi-Fi connection to avoid the temptation of being online for one reason or another.

Likewise, assess your social media presence. Which social media platform would you like to be on, how often should you be accessing it and how can you regulate the time you spend on it? I am not on Facebook, Twitter or Instagram, but then maybe I'm an ancient relic in this regard.

Further, as you move from one focus area to another or one meeting to the other, you can follow a transition ritual. Get closure on the first task—make notes of what you need to do or follow up on so you don't have any lingering thoughts about it. As you begin the second task or meeting, centre yourself again. Acknowledge your feelings at the time (worried, anxious, fearful, excited), remind yourself to leave all those feelings aside for the next thirty minutes and commit to being fully present for the activity on hand.

You can also build your capacity for focusing on the present by practising it during your day-to-day, routine activities. Focus on brushing your teeth while brushing your teeth (rather than on the plans for the day); enjoy your shower more fully by experiencing the flow of water on your skin, feeling the release of tiredness from your body and connecting with feeling refreshed and nourished; read the morning paper without simultaneously gulping down breakfast and browsing overnight political updates online.

2. Learning to let go

Mindfulness is about being more balanced, and it's quite impossible to be emotionally balanced when you are out of balance in the physical space. If you want to focus more fully on the present and invest in deepening your self-awareness, you need to be less rushed. This requires learning to let go. Be clear on your choices, prioritise and be willing to let go of certain opportunities. Creating empty spaces in your schedule will allow you to be more reflective and connect with your inner stillness. You can then be more present and mindful with whatever you are engaged in.

Our inability to focus on the present moment is closely linked with our attachment to outcomes. We desperately want only specific and favourable results and are uncomfortable with other possibilities. We obsess over outcomes and our odds of achieving them. This makes it harder to let go. To mindfully engage with the present, you need to be invested in the process and not the outcomes. I know what you are thinking: in a cutthroat, competitive business environment, how can you lose track of outcomes? I am not suggesting you don't track your outcomes. What I am recommending is to not obsess about the short-term outcomes of your actions. If you stay focused on the process, and do the right things, the appropriate results will follow. Sometimes those results may be slightly different from your expectations, at other times they may take longer than your desire—but they will manifest.

In order to let go of the fixation with results, you also need to have faith in something bigger than yourself. We need to appreciate that the universe is evolving perfectly at all times. The sun rises and sets as it needs to, different weathers arrive and pass as they need to and plants are born—some to become trees and some to die early—as they need to. The universe is also unfolding in our life, as it needs to. It is we humans who often resist it. Seized by our insecure mind, we get attached to certain outcomes in the strong belief that those outcomes are necessarily better than any other possibilities. Learning to go with the flow of the universe and accepting that whatever happens, happens for our highest good, slows down our thought patterns and helps us be more centred in the present.

3. Being a self-observer

Moment to moment self-awareness is integral to being mindful. Only when you are aware of your shifting thoughts and inner feelings, can you catch yourself being reactive and make the shift to being responsive. If you are conscious in the moment when you just start to feel hurt by someone's critical comments, you have a better chance of not taking them personally. You give yourself the opportunity to respond in a balanced and assertive way. Similarly, consider a situation where, as the CEO of your company, you are actively trying to acquire another business. If you are observant of your inner being, you will have a clearer insight into your true motivations for this aspiration. You'll know how much of your desire is emanating from the likely benefit to your customers and employees, how much from the hope of greater profitability and how much from your egoistic pursuit to run a bigger empire. Being in touch with the true motivation might facilitate you in making a better quality decision.

Our body-mind is mysteriously powerful. Once we consistently shine light on our wholistic experience, from what's happening in our body to our inner thoughts and feelings, our body-mind automatically starts making healthier choices. We don't need to force it in any way—when you are aware of an injured right arm, your left arm starts to compensate for it. Let's say you are working towards eliminating your tendency to be angry. As you cultivate mindfulness, you start to become aware of the rising emotions of tension, frustration and anger within you before you actually become angry or display it. This awareness is where the greatest opportunity for change lies. Firstly, this awareness, coupled with some willpower to make new choices, will pave the way for you to, hopefully, not act from that place of anger. Secondly, if you can routinely be aware of these emotions as soon as they arise and not get attached to them, they will start to subside on their own.

One important consideration in developing the practice of enhancing self-awareness can dramatically impact the benefit you receive: it is key that when you become aware of any thought or emotion within, you merely observe it without judging the thought or judging yourself. Feelings are packets of transitory energy. They arise and pass away. Judging them strengthens their hold on you. In the above example of anger, if you were to judge yourself and get upset every time you experience those feelings, they would solidify. They may even get supplemented by feelings of self-hatred and lower self-esteem. Merely observing your feelings, however, without judging them, dilutes their power over you and assists in letting them pass.

4. Mindfulness meditation

Meditation is the discovery that the point of life is always arrived at in the present moment.

– ALAN WATTS, British-born philosopher

Besides practising the above ideas in your everyday life, I would urge you to consider building a regular practice of mindfulness meditation. Such a practice builds muscle memory; it trains your body and mind to respond rather than react in different situations.

We've already discussed meditation and its benefits in Insight 4. Mindfulness meditation is a specific meditation technique that trains you to focus on the present so you can become more aware of your thoughts and feelings and acknowledge them without judging them. One of the most established mindfulness meditation practices is to, with your eyes closed, focus your attention on your breath. You can notice and feel the breath either just below the nostrils or with the rise and fall of your stomach. As you try to focus on the breath, invariably, within moments, you would get distracted and be lost in your thoughts. As soon as you realise that, acknowledge it, and without judging yourself or your thoughts, bring your attention back to your breath.

Directing your attention in this way quietens the mind and sharpens its focus. The quieter the mind, the more reflective it becomes and that, in turn, allows for greater clarity to emerge. Breath is always in the present; we are only ever breathing the current breath, never the previous or the next one. Thus, concentrating on the breath helps us be centered and in the present. Experiencing such centredness and quietness within is empowering. As you practise this technique over time, you can significantly raise the level of your concentration in any given moment, resulting in greater focus and productivity in whatever you may be engaged in. Lastly, the practice of not judging our thoughts, distractions or ourselves during meditation enhances our ability to be non-judgmental the rest of the day as well.

The key to cultivating mindfulness is to build a consistent practice. Practice these ideas regularly by making them a part of your daily life.

Personal actions

1. Reflect on how mindful or distracted you tend to be. What impact does this have on your leadership effectiveness, relationships, ability to enjoy the moment and level of happiness and fulfilment?
2. Reflect on the ideal state of mindfulness for yourself. What would be different about you then? What difference would leading and living from this state make to you? What, specifically, would you like to start doing towards cultivating greater mindfulness? How would you track your progress?

Applying the *Inside-Out* Approach: Wisdom and Balance

Insight 15

From Workaholism and Disharmony to Wholistic Well-being and Balance

To go beyond is as wrong as to fall short.

— CONFUCIUS, Chinese philosopher

GAUTAMA BUDDHA WAS BORN RICH BUT SOON REALISED THAT MATERIAL possessions did not make him happy. He sacrificed all the comforts of his palace and became an ascetic so he could focus on spiritual growth. He conducted intense experiments with his body and mind, at times depriving himself of even food and sleep. After six years of persevering with this approach, he felt that this too did not make him truly happy.

He then decided to meditate on the truth of human existence. Reflection showed him that both these approaches, seeking only materialism or only asceticism, were extreme steps and hence flawed. It was while meditating by a river that he was struck with the realisation about the need for balance. Enamoured by a lute player in a passing boat, he had a sudden burst of insight. He recognised that for the lute to produce beautiful and harmonious sound, the strings needed to be tuned just right—neither too taut nor too slack. If they were strung too tight, the instrument would produce a shrill noise; if they were strung too slack, it would produce a dull sound. That's how he started practising and, later, preaching the 'middle way'.

Put simply, the middle way is the idea that in order to progress effectively on the human journey of evolution, we need a healthy balance between extremes. It is rooted in the notion that, even a virtue when practised in excess, becomes a vice; that too much of a good thing is not necessarily good. Though the catalyst for Buddha's realisation was the need to find balance between self-indulgence and self-mortification, this is a powerful idea that we can apply to any aspect of our life. The notion of the 'sweet spot' in my first book, *Discovering Your Sweet Spot*, relates to discovering a similar optimal balance between the paradoxical opposites of our life.

The human body and mind are a microcosm of the universe. Just as different aspects of nature (birth and death, sunrise and sunset and the earth's rotation around the sun) need to be in balance, the human body and mind need to stay aligned to their natural rhythms to operate optimally. Our body works on the principle of homeostasis, the maintenance of equilibrium of different bodily functions for an optimal functioning of the whole. This requires appropriate levels of body temperature, body fluids, minerals and salts, blood sugar and so forth. If any of these are out of sync, we fall ill. The body then fights the illness to bring the different elements back into balance. If the healthy interaction and flow of information among the body's cells is disturbed for a prolonged time, it can lead to chronic, and sometimes life-threatening, diseases.

Likewise, a key condition for an optimal experience of life's journey is a healthy balance in different aspects of our being. This includes finding balance between work and life, physical health and emotional well-being, receiving and giving, goal-orientation and people-orientation, professional growth and personal relationships, passion and detachment, success and happiness and so on. If you are a high-performing leader or want to become one, getting this right is crucial for you. Imbalance in these opposing forces would create a disturbance in your state of being, and that is bound to impact the quality of your leadership. If you are not healthy or don't enjoy loving relationships at home or are unhappy, it is hard to imagine you sustaining peak performance at work over an extended period of time. Similarly, being organised without flexibility makes you rigid, being flexible without organisation makes you defocused; being direct in your communication without tact makes you appear harsh, being tactful without authenticity makes you appear deceptive; being driven without stress-management skills can burn you out, mastering stress-management without enough drive can make you complacent.

You also need balance among the various dimensions of leadership that we have discussed in the previous chapters. For example, while I accentuated the importance of strategic orientation over operational excellence (Insight 4) or of choosing the kind of leader you want to *be* over things you need to *do* as a leader (Insight 11), eventually you require a healthy balance between these. Similarly, while direction (Insight 12) is of primary importance, you don't want to ignore distance completely. The reason I have emphasised one side of these equations is because that's where I find most leaders have a greater opportunity to grow. Having said that, in this chapter, I would like to draw your attention to a sense of balance as it's applicable to your life as a leader—not just at work, but in a more comprehensive way. Let's explore the opportunity for greater balance in some of the key facets of your life as a leader.

Professional and personal life

Bronnie Ware, an Australian nurse, spent several years working in palliative care, looking after patients in the last weeks of their lives. She recorded their dying insights in a book called *The Top Five Regrets of the Dying*. One of the top regrets expressed by them was, 'I wish I had not worked so hard.'

Work might be terribly important to you, and you may even be involved in some path-breaking pursuits, but not paying attention to your well-being, personal relationships or other personal interests doesn't serve you well in the long run. Ask yourself what's most important to you in life: among other themes, health, happiness and relationships are likely to be strong candidates for inclusion in that list. All good things in life take time to build. So does developing health, relationships and happiness skills. As we age, what we long for are better health and well-being. However, a body that has been abused by overwork, lack of exercise, regular jet lag and limited sleep is a challenge to mend. Research shows that in old age, a majority of the affluent are very willing to trade a large proportion of their wealth for a few extra years. They wish they had been more mindful of taking care of their health in their earlier years. Similarly, one of the biggest regrets I hear some of my older clients describe is the limited time they were able to devote to their children. Not only do they miss enjoying their kids' childhood now, but also feel the unstated distance in their relationship. Think about this: when your children are adults, what would they say was most important to you while they were growing up? I am sure it would break your heart if they said it was your work.

Investing in your well-being, relationships and personal interests not only keeps you balanced and happy, but it also helps you become a stronger and well-adjusted leader. As someone said, 'You can't do a good job if your job is all you do.' If you work from home, you have to be particularly mindful of this advice. As much as working from home offers greater flexibility to create adequate family and personal time, many leaders struggle with establishing that balance. For them, with no clear demarcation between work and home, work simply overflows into personal time. It's essential that you design non-negotiable time windows in your day to exercise, reflect, pursue personal interests and enjoy time with the family.

From measuring output to measuring productivity

For you to initiate any meaningful balance between your professional and personal life, you have to be sharply focused on productivity. That means constantly being mindful of your output to input ratio—measuring the amount and quality of your efforts and the quality of your outcomes. Ordinarily, in a leadership position, you are likely to feel pressured to maximise output. However, smarter leaders focus as much on maximising productivity. Are you working really hard to merely keep the lights of your division on, or are you clearly steering the division in a strategic direction? What are the common causes for your productivity leakage—lack of resources, under-utilisation of existing resources or low reliance on the latest technological tools? What personality traits—perfectionism, discomfort trusting the team to deliver with limited supervision, an inability to say 'No' to a new opportunity—come in the way of your being more productive? When was the last time you pushed back on an idea that offered promise but did not align with your strategic vision? At what level of input does your productivity start to decline? If you work an hour less every day, by how much would your output decline? Have you considered building the mindset of maximising output in a fixed number of working hours instead of stretchable hours?

Reflecting on such questions can support you in determining the optimum level of effort that you need to incur at work for strong and strategic results.

From what you do to who you are

At a deeper level, the imbalance between professional and personal life stems from a strong identification with work. When your self-image is defined by what you do—the title and the role you have at work—it creates a vicious cycle. The more you identify with your work, the more you invest time and energy in it; the more time you invest in it, the more it defines your self-image. Clearly unhealthy, this loop distorts your sense of self, makes you obsess about work and increases the imbalance in your life. Arguably, if you lead an NGO, you may believe that your single-minded pursuit is only benefitting society, and is hence reasonable. However, the need for balance transcends that. Balance is as much a need of the universe as it is of the individual, and by not serving this innate need, you are, in a way, adding to the imbalance of the universe.

What you require is to let go of this attachment to work and discover your fuller self. You have to stop relating to yourself based only on what you do and start connecting with who you are. You are a multifaceted being. You not only have multiple roles in society, from being a child and a parent to a responsible social citizen, but also have a higher purpose to fulfil. As we discussed in Insight 12, a part of your purpose is the work you do on yourself. As long as you remain preoccupied with only one dimension of your life, even if it is dedicated to a meaningful cause, you will struggle to stay connected with the path of self-realisation and personal mastery.

Wholistic well-being

Well-being can be misjudged. You can have a unidimensional relationship with well-being. Some leaders are highly disciplined about their daily workout. They religiously carry their kit wherever they travel. A day without a workout is incomplete for them. There are others who live by the belief that emotional well-being is the key to health. As long as they feel good, surround themselves with loving relationships and engage in activities that enhance that feeling, they believe they are likely to be healthy, happy and sleep well. While each of these approaches is an expression of a positive relationship with well-being, neither is complete in itself. What you need is a well-balanced and wholistic approach to well-being that responds to your physical, emotional, mental and spiritual needs. Such wholistic well-being is essential to the journey of personal mastery—the real pathway to shift from good to great.

Attending to physical health is obviously important. You need a healthy body to take on the physical demands of your leadership role. All the same, physical health must be understood and addressed in a balanced way. There are three foundational aspects of a healthy body—nutrition, exercise and sleep. Nutrition directly correlates to the quality of fuel for your body. Not only do you need to eat healthy, but you also need to ensure that your diet is balanced enough to provide your body the necessary intake of proteins, carbohydrates, fats, vitamins and minerals. All ancient health systems, like Ayurveda and traditional Chinese medicine, recognise each body to be different and recommend nutrition and diet that are tailored to your specific body type. This is pertinent to note in the context of the innumerable diet fads that exist today and that many leaders feel drawn to follow.

Similarly, a wholistic approach to exercise assumes adequate attention to building all the four facets of fitness: stamina, strength, flexibility and balance. Each of these requires different forms of exercise—from aerobic exercises and weight-training to yoga and Pilates. You need to ideally create a healthy mix of these in your fitness regimen. Lastly, an appropriate amount and quality of sleep is vital. If you are routinely getting insufficient or disturbed sleep, be mindful that it may be a warning sign of an underlying deterioration in health. In an overdrive mode of leadership, it is easy to consider sleep a 'hurdle'. If only it could be avoided, it would give you more hours! On the contrary, all elite performers, including top athletes who are used to repeatedly performing at their peak, lay great emphasis on rest and recovery. Stretching yourself beyond your comfort zone develops new muscles only when high levels of activity are followed by adequate rest. Rest and sleep allow the body to rebuild damaged cells and recover its rhythm to take on more the next day.

Emotional well-being includes nurturing a healthy self-esteem, strong resilience and wholesome relationships. A healthy self-esteem implies a balanced view of yourself. That means neither having a superficially high opinion nor a misplaced low opinion of yourself; neither do you always blame others for setbacks nor do you instinctively blame yourself. Likewise, emotional well-being is a balance between being adept at managing your emotions and expressing them fully. If you suppress your feelings, they become a drain on your well-being. All the same, if you are not mindful in choosing which emotions to express or how to express them, you can easily hurt others. Striking such balance is key to forming and nurturing wholesome professional and personal relationships. Investing in meaningful relationships where you can be yourself, learning to share your feelings and being willing to be vulnerable and building a more loving and compassionate relationship with yourself, and with others, can enhance your emotional well-being. Pursuing activities that are emotionally fulfilling for you, such as sports or creative hobbies, time in nature or with friends, or time serving in the community, aid your sense of balance, emotional connect and ground you.

Mental well-being, too, is a balancing act. It's the balance between intelligence and judgment, determination and acceptance, optimism and realism, ambition and flexibility, expertise and willingness to learn, strength and humility. Being skewed towards any one of these paradoxical opposites warps your sense of reality. You then tend to struggle to reconcile your perception of reality with objective reality. For example, if you are an expert but unwilling to learn, you stop growing. On the other hand, if you simply love learning but don't harness it towards gaining expertise or applying it to real-life issues, your knowledge may be less valuable. Similarly, if you are strong and capable but lack humility, you would be less accepted and less liked by your colleagues; if you are humble but are not strong enough to take a stand, you risk your views being ignored. Reflecting regularly, meditating, reading a variety of texts and engaging with people from diverse backgrounds and views can keep you healthy and balanced in this regard.

Lastly, spiritual well-being is about nourishing your soul. If the most enduring part of you is not getting fulfilled, you are unlikely to experience deeper peace. Without that, your personal and professional effectiveness is bound to be compromised. Staying connected with your deeper personal values, progressing on the path of your life's higher purpose, pursuing your calling and continuing to evolve as a human being are the cornerstones of spiritual well-being. Cultivate greater acceptance, of yourself and others; develop a non-judgmental awareness of all situations; and learn to be grateful to further your spiritual growth. Be kind to others and serve a cause greater than yourself to nourish the soul.

Giving and receiving

Receiving without giving is like trying to breathe without exhaling. Unless we exhale fully, our body becomes toxic. We need balance between receiving and accumulation on one side and giving and sharing on the other.

As an ambitious leader of a corporate business, there's a reasonable risk that you may become self-absorbed and narrowly focused on your individual and business goals. It is also easy to get attached to your success and be caught up in the rewards and recognition it brings. In the process, you can take your blessings for granted and become disconnected with the plight of the less privileged. It's not because you don't care, it's because you are consumed by the whirlwind of professional activity. It's not that you don't intend to give back, but with paucity of time, you conveniently postpone real action to a later date.

Human beings like to be generous. When you are kind and giving, not only does the other person benefit from your generosity, but you feel good and fulfilled as well. This holds especially true when you help others in the forms of acts, such as participating as a volunteer with an NGO, rather than through passive means, such as writing a check.

Furthermore, understanding your intent behind the act of giving is important. As the law of karma suggests, intentions are most vital. When you give with the motivation of fulfilling a personal desire—maybe of looking good among your social network or demonstrating to others how generous you are—you are still not earning good karma. As long as it's still about you, if anything, you are only building on your existing baggage of karma linked to egoistic desires of success, power, fame and social approval. When you give with the pure intent to help and share, on the other hand, irrespective of the size of giving, you earn good karma.

In the journey of personal mastery, as you connect with your true inner self and feel grateful for your life, you automatically feel more loving, kind and empathetic towards others. You then don't give back because you should or you have to, but because you want to. The question is how connected are you with your true inner self? How drawn do you feel towards helping others? What specific steps can you take to bridge the gap between your intentions and actions?

In a leadership position, you have an enormous canvas for giving. Giving can start from the little things—besides being kind to your colleagues, you can be more generous towards your junior staff, blue collar workers and personal assistants. Further, you and your team can get involved with various community activities, both in your personal or professional capacity. Equally significantly, you can be mindful of the social impact of every decision and action of your team and organisation. What's the social benefit of the products or services you offer? Do your organisation's policies, in any way, risk exacerbating social ills, such as the use of child labour, poor working conditions and lack of diversity and inclusion, or worsening climate change? What good is huge business growth if it comes at enormous social costs, including destroying the very planet we live on?

Success, happiness and fulfilment

At the end of the day, everyone wants to be happy. All the same, our actions are not always aligned to this objective. We seek inner happiness but assume its path is via outer rewards of money and success. While success and material progress contribute to happiness, they are not the most significant factors. The road to happiness is an independent one that overlaps with success only for the initial part of the journey. After a certain level of success, its correlation with happiness veers off. Having travelled on the overlapping tracks initially, we begin to believe that the correlation is permanent. We then blindly chase money and success, and lose sight of the law of diminishing returns. We also underestimate the role of happiness in becoming successful—you are likely to be more successful at what you are happy doing. We need to acquire different life skills for the two tracks. Both take time, effort and energy, which is why the need for balance. As we become better at both, we ensure they intertwine again. Success can, once again, contribute to happiness and happiness to success.

Happiness is an attitude. It is a state of being. I am sure you can think of someone in your life, among your family, friends or colleagues, who's generally always happy. What is it about them that allows them to be this way? I would assume that they have their set of challenges, but how come they don't get bogged down? Happier people have one thing in common. It's not that they have perfect lives, but that they are at peace with the imperfections in their life. While some people may be natural at this state of being, I believe each of us can build the skills to be happier.

Happiness is the ultimate balancing act. In our continued journey of personal mastery, being happier requires that we arrive at a balanced view about the fundamental dilemmas of our life—the tussle between material growth and spiritual progress, and between actualizing professional and human potential. Material progress without spiritual growth lacks meaning, understanding and wisdom; spiritual growth without skills for material progress can leave you ill-equipped to furnish your full range of responsibilities in life. Concentrating primarily on maximising bodily pleasures can leave you weak in character; but then nurturing your soul by denying the physical body may not leave you with enough physical strength to pursue spirituality. Single-mindedly chasing success, without any connection to a deeper purpose, lacks fulfilment; on the other hand, pursuing a purposeful path without building skills to be successful leads to frustration and feelings of inadequacy.

As you immerse yourself in your work, you may rationalise your commitment as a drive to actualise your professional potential. You want to see how far you can go, how outstanding you can become, as a professional. That seems like a worthy pursuit. However, you must view it in the light of the opportunity you may have in discovering and actualising your full human potential—and that may be bigger than merely your professional potential. Becoming the best at what you do is not necessarily a reflection of the best you can be as a person. Just because you succeed professionally does not, in any way, indicate how self-aware, kind, non-judgmental, courageous, nurturing, generous or mindful you are. In what way could you evolve as a spouse, parent, citizen and as a human being? Balancing professional growth with personal growth in this way can create better conditions for happiness and fulfilment in your life.

In that respect, happiness and fulfilment are natural by products of the journey of personal mastery and *Inside-Out* leadership. They are the culmination of achieving a healthy balance and harmony across the various dimensions of your being.

Personal actions

1. Reflect on the quality of the balance between your professional and personal life as well as among the physical, emotional, mental and

spiritual aspects of your well-being. What do you need to change in order to create a better balance?

2. How has your involvement with the social sector been? What social causes are you most drawn to? What opportunities do you see to be able to contribute more actively towards these causes?

3. What changes do you need to make to create a better balance between the different dimensions of your life (material and spiritual growth, fulfilling professional potential and human potential and success and happiness)?

Insight 16

From Quick Wins
to Lasting Change

One can choose to go back toward safety or forward toward growth.
Growth must be chosen again and again; fear must be overcome again
and again.

— ABRAHAM MASLOW, psychologist

I ACKNOWLEDGE YOU FOR MAKING IT THIS FAR INTO THE BOOK. THAT'S already a strong statement of your intent and commitment to explore ways to enhance your leadership and personal effectiveness. I hope that as you read through the book, you could resonate with the insights shared, and could identify some potential areas to work on. Now comes the second part of the challenge: *converting intent into action.* You must manifest the ideas you have for your self-improvement into actual reality. Equally important is that you sustain the positive changes so they become a part of you. As we all know, the road to hell is paved with good intentions. Making those intentions come alive and steadily imbibing new approaches in your personality is the whole point of the exercise. Here are some key aspects of this process that I would like to share with you.

Build an action plan

As you read through the book, did you get the chance to work with the personal actions listed at the end of each Insight? If you did, you probably have a list of action items ready to be worked on. If not, I strongly urge you to revisit those actions at the end of each chapter, or make such a list independently. The list will likely have a spectrum of ideas—from quick-fixes to deeper personality shifts, from a weekly plan to long-term goals to build your inner strength and resilience. While you may be tempted to initially work only on the low-hanging fruits, I recommend including at least a couple of the deeper shifts in your active plan as well. This protects you from forever postponing the most significant opportunities for development. Besides, many of your goals will be interrelated. Sometimes, working on some of the long-term shifts supports the progress you're making on the more immediate ones; for example, being curious about others and accepting them as they are might make the execution of your plan to have a monthly lunch with your colleagues more fruitful. All the same, you want to make your plan specific, bite-size and actionable. You could break down bigger and more long-term goals into mini-goals. For example, to make a shift from a captain style to a coaching style of leadership, you could initially focus only on one of the key traits you would like to develop, such as enhancing your listening skills. You can then add another one, say, a deliberate focus on asking questions instead of providing solutions.

Making your plan as specific as possible is a recipe for greater success. Visualise yourself living your plan and then capture the specifics of that scenario. If you are planning to exercise three to four times a week, a specific and actionable plan might say, 'Run and exercise in the gym for forty-five minutes, starting at 7.30 a.m., on Tuesdays and Thursdays; play tennis with friends on Saturdays around 5 p.m.; go for a walk with my partner on Sundays around 6 p.m.' This may have other follow-on actions. For example, if you don't have access to a gym currently, maybe you want to become a member of one, or perhaps you want to reactivate your tennis buddy group and so on.

When making your action plan, you may also like to pay attention to expressing your action items in a positive slant. As I highlighted in Insight 8 with regard to designing positive affirmations, instead of putting down 'avoid being permissive' as an action item, reframe it as, 'choose to be assertive'; in place of 'stop being directive', choose 'be more empowering'. When you reinforce your action plan in the negative, it keeps you focused on the limiting trait, and your mind will subconsciously act out the behaviour that you are consciously reminding it of. As Socrates wisely remarked, 'The secret of change is to focus all of your energy, not on fighting the old, but on building the new.' Neurological research suggests that it is easier to introduce new wiring in the brain than fix an old one. So, instead of fighting old instincts that we want to change, it is better to experience what new instincts could feel like and try to repeat that experience.

Start where you are

Another important consideration in initiating your action plan is not to wait for an imaginary perfect time—a time when you have the bandwidth, the mind space and the time to embark on the journey of change. Remember, 'perfect' can be the enemy of progress. Choosing perfection is like choosing to be happy at a later date. It's the equivalent of putting your happiness, effectiveness and fulfilment on hold so that you can get through a busy phase. As a leader, be wary of this dangerous trap. You are unlikely to find that golden period when you are not busy, not involved with an important project or agenda, or not dealing with a significant change in your ecosystem. Undoubtedly, sometimes the list of personal changes can seem overwhelming. Break them down into bite-sized action items, if required. As we discussed, whether it's empowering the team or building your inner strength, there are small steps you can start on right away. Don't let those opportunities slide.

Be intentional in your practice and discipline

Being intentional about the changes you decide to pursue is important. That means you mentally commit to your action plan and stay connected with it on a regular basis. If you wish to alter your relationship with one of your senior directors, it requires reminding yourself about the approach or attitude you need to bring to the conversation before every interaction with that individual. Similarly, if you are learning to 'let go' more actively, be deliberate about finding opportunities in the day to practise it. This could take the form of letting go of the need to perfect your presentation, taming your tendency of excessively following up on your colleagues or the compulsion to constantly check your inbox. Being intentional also involves reviewing your thoughts, actions and behaviours after the event. Was I a good listener? Was I open-minded? Was I non-judgemental during our meeting? (Assuming those are the traits you would like to build.) As you practice new behaviours in such commonplace scenarios, you'll find adapting to change becomes easier.

Being intentional raises your level of self-awareness and makes you more conscious of the desired behaviour when the situation actually arises. It aids in pre-programming your mind to approach situations in the desired way, so you are not hostage to your habitual patterns. Even if you fall into the trap of past instincts, there's a high chance you will become aware of it sooner. If you were unable to watch your anger in the heat of the moment, you will likely remind yourself of the slippage at least after it happened.

Being intentional necessitates a certain level of disciplined approach to the journey of change. You need to create some kind of tracker of your intentions and progress. You could review your tracker on a daily basis, at least in the early stages of the journey, or on a weekly basis. You could even make a quick note in your phone after every situation that tests your behaviour. Let's say you intend to practise saying 'no' to less important priorities in your day-to-day life—start with recording every time you say no (or every time you don't say 'no') when you should have. Reviewing this list at the end of the day or week can assist you in staying very aware of the progress and slowly rewire your brain to remember to do something about it in the future. You can even consider giving yourself a daily score on your performance against each of your action plan items. When you are trying to inculcate a new habit, especially in the early stages, measuring your *effort* is more important than measuring outcomes. Your intention and effort is entirely in your control. Review how well you're trying to stay true to your intention. This can support you in staying focused on your efforts, even if they don't yield the results you are seeking in the beginning. The results will surely follow.

Engage a partner

Another practice that's helpful when trying to stay on top of your journey of change is to engage a partner in keeping you accountable. You could consider one or more of your colleagues, your spouse, your children or a friend for the job. The objective is for them to check in with you at a predetermined frequency, say, once every fifteen days, about how you are doing with respect to each of your chosen goals. You can also encourage them to ask you a couple of additional questions, such as, what helped you or what came in the way and what you are going to do in the coming week to progress on your goal. This serves to raise your level of accountability. You must clarify to your partner that while they check on your progress, they should not assess or judge you in any way nor offer you any unsolicited suggestions. Their role is merely to ask you how well you did, what helped or did not help and what you need to do in the following fortnight.

Establish early wins

Motivating yourself works much the same way as motivating your colleagues. Establishing early wins is crucial to building confidence and momentum around any initiative. Often, the hardest part of the journey is to get off the block. The late Stephen Covey described this phenomenon with the example of Apollo 11's historic voyage to the moon in 1969. The astronauts, Neil Armstrong and Buzz Aldrin, left earth and travelled more than 800,000 kilometres in space to make the journey to the moon. Fascinating and inspiring as it was, guess which part of the journey consumed the largest amount of energy? It wasn't landing on the moon or even the spacecraft's long journey to the moon. It was the *lift-off* from the surface of earth. That alone consumed more power and energy than the rest of the journey put together. The example is a powerful reminder of the importance of the initial push to get started in our efforts to break old habits.

Like the gravitational pull of the earth, the hold of our old habitual patterns is quite strong. In coaching parlance, on a scale of zero to ten, moving from zero to one is infinitely harder than moving from six to seven. But breaking through can be as liberating as landing on the moon! Once you graduate to one, you are a big step closer to accomplishing your goals. From thereon, the effects of positive change can be addictive. When you experience the benefits, for example, of deeper relationships by learning to be assertive and authentic or of higher quality family time by being more strategic in your office, you will want to build on them and sustain them.

One of my clients, Sushmita, is a seasoned management consultant and routinely follows the 80:80 rule for inculcating a new habit. Her approach is to aim to complete the activity at least 80 per cent of the time, with at least 80 per cent satisfaction level. So, if the target is to go for a 5 km run, five times a week, she is happy if she runs for 4 kms at least four times a week. It is a good way to stretch yourself without being too hard on yourself as you build a new routine.

Treat it as a journey

Change can be difficult. It's challenging to alter patterns that we've built over the years. Our personality traits, of aggression, anger, insecurity, perfectionism, envy or obsession, are so deep-rooted in our psyche that it's not easy to dislodge them. Not only does doing so take a lot of conscious effort, but also energy and stamina. In that sense, you should treat most significant positive shifts as a journey, not a one-off event. Personal mastery is not a destination; it's a journey that we commit to. It's not about somehow losing five kilos of weight once, but about becoming fitter for life. In order to reduce by a few inches, you could go on a crash diet or exercise heavily for a few months. Invariably, such attempts, while impressive at first, do not have a lasting effect. You gain those inches back in a few months. Being healthy and fit on a sustained basis requires creating a new relationship with your body. It requires embracing a new attitude towards food, exercise and well-being. You then begin to recognise the need to take care of your health, rather than treat your body as a machine that is meant to serve your mind's desires. You connect with the food you eat not merely for its pleasurable taste on the tongue, but also for its nutritional value. Exercise is no longer a chore, but a fun and invigorating break in the day. All these shifts emanate from a continued exploration of yourself and understanding what raises your personal performance at work and life. As you consider this to be a journey, you don't relate to every positive milestone along the way as an end in itself, but merely an affirmation of the ongoing process.

Understand how change works

They say practice makes perfect. Actually, it's the right practice that makes perfect; you need to know how to practise correctly for it to be the most effective. Likewise, willpower, focus and discipline are essential for any journey of change. Once again, an understanding of the mechanics of change will help boost your confidence and resilience. You then have greater awareness of what to expect and are better prepared to deal with setbacks when they arrive.

To get you started on this journey, let's discuss the four stages of competence linked with learning any new skill—a model conceptualised by Martin Broadwell, a management trainer. If you refer to the diagram below, you will see the four stages are essentially four possible combinations of high or low levels of consciousness and competence.

Four stages of competence

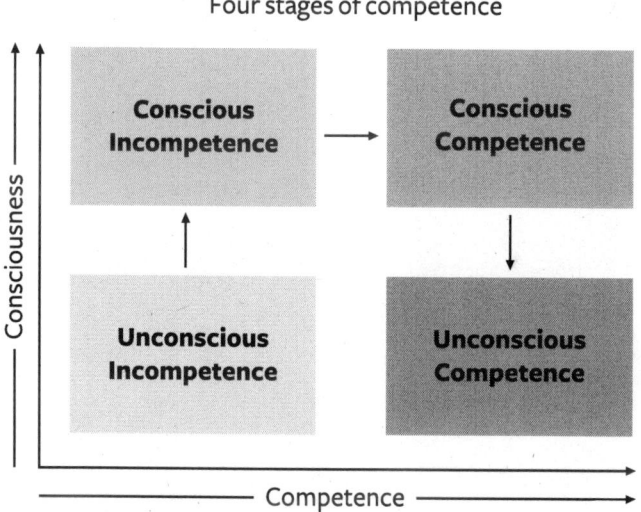

Most journeys of change start with the stage of *Unconscious Incompetence*. This is your blind spot, where you are unaware of a limiting personal trait, although in many cases it's very visible to others.

Ranjan was a highly competent sales director of a pharmaceutical company. He was seen to have high potential and was being considered for the MD position. He was a high-energy leader and actively contributed to meetings with his MD and other directors. But he was perplexed when his MD mentioned something about him not being well-liked by his peers.

The second stage is *Conscious Incompetence*. In this stage, you are aware of your limitation. Maybe you receive feedback from a colleague or a family member.

As part of his leadership development, Ranjan went through a 360-degree feedback. From the feedback, it was clear that he was perceived as a pushy and dominating leader. His peers also felt that he was insensitive to their views and feelings during various interactions. He discussed the feedback with his MD, who emphasised the importance of Ranjan addressing this issue. He also highlighted that this was crucial if he wished to be considered for the MD's role in the future. After the initial phase of denial and disbelief, Ranjan acknowledged the feedback and was keen to do something about it. Through coaching conversations, he explored how else could he be with his peers, and zeroed in on a few different ideas. He wished to be a better listener, improve his listening to talking ratio, acknowledge and encourage others' contributions, be patient and not rush to conclusions and connect with his colleagues not just on a rational but on an emotional level too.

As he started to practise these ideas, he moved to the third stage—*Conscious Competence*. This stage is the toughest of the four. This is where the rubber hits the road. Here, you experience the challenge and the frustration of being unable to let go of your deeply ingrained habits. Besides, sticking to the chosen plan is not easy. You may occasionally slip into the second stage, the stage of 'Conscious Incompetence', where you are aware of what you should be doing, but don't end up doing it.

It took Ranjan more than a few months of conscious practice to improve his listening and be more considerate of his colleagues.

These efforts can initially feel unnatural and come across as a bit clunky. If you have never complimented a colleague on their contribution, it's going to seem strange the first few times. However, if you stick to the plan and genuinely persevere with the changes, irrespective of some slippages on the way, you move to the final stage—the stage of *Unconscious Competence*. This stage comes when you have been practising your new thinking or behaviour so consistently, it's now become a new habit. It's so well ingrained in your being that you no longer need to be conscious of it or remind yourself to be that way.

> Besides trying to alter his behaviour, Ranjan examined his beliefs about true leadership. He also grasped the importance of people, at work and in his personal life, as opposed to goals and achievements. After nine months of persistent effort, the MD felt that Ranjan was far more ready for his next role.

Through these steps, it's important to stay connected with your inner journey as well. When you relate to the underlying thoughts and emotions at different stages of this competence map, you become more sensitised to your own negative triggers and derailers as well as your thoughts and beliefs that support you in those situations. As you stay conscious of the circumstances that accelerate your slippages, the beliefs that help you get back on track, the emotional experience of overcoming the challenges, the regrets about not sticking to your plan and the sense of accomplishment in achieving a personal goal, you greatly deepen your self-awareness and accelerate your journey of change.

Sustain the journey

Although we touched on the notion of unconscious competence, it's important that you identify and practise approaches that help you sustain positive change. Recently, I was delivering a talk to a group of business leaders in Singapore. During the Q&A session, someone from the audience asked me a wonderful question: 'Now that your vocation has become a successful business, how connected are you with your personal purpose that guided you to this path to begin with?'

Discovering your sweet spot is one thing, sustaining it is another ball game altogether. To get to number one ranking in tennis is hard, but staying there? That's even harder. I've seen it happen from time to time—the passion and sense of purpose of start-up founders diminishes with success, organisations get caught up in the numbers game as they scale up and individuals get busy and complacent with their progress.

Sustaining change is akin to cultivating the mindset of an elite performer. Elite performers, whether in the field of sports, performing arts or in business, have a process of continuous self-improvement in place that supports them in building a long-lasting and high-performance career. They surround themselves with experts from different fields. As the leader of an organisation, don't limit yourself to subject-matter experts in various functions, such as technology, marketing, sales and finance, related to your organisational domain, but surround yourself with thought leaders from other fields, such as academia, strategy consulting, executive coaching, civil society and health and well-being, as well as peers from other industries. Create your personal advisory board. That's how you can stay abreast with the latest thinking in all these areas and that directly contributes towards continuous improvement.

Further, seek feedback from colleagues and family members from time to time, about how you can continue to improve; this serves to keep you on the journey of mastery. In addition, make room for structured and quality reflection time in your daily and weekly routine. A steady reflective practice can form the foundation that supports you in creating such a process for self-improvement, taking stock of your progress and continually refreshing your process.

Endnote

Be mindful that the pursuit of these changes is part of the overall ongoing journey of personal mastery. The path to such mastery is the cornerstone of all remarkable personal and leadership transformation. This is what *Inside-Out* leadership is about. This is what creates truly great leadership.

I believe each of us has the opportunity to raise our leadership and personal effectiveness, and experience greater success, balance, happiness and fulfilment in our lives by investing in deepening our self-awareness, taking greater personal responsibility of all our thoughts, emotions and actions and living the higher purpose we were born to live!

Personal actions

1. Finalise your action plan. What are your key goals? What specifically do you need to start doing to achieve these? How do you intend to phase them in so you can pay appropriate attention to them?
2. How committed are you to this plan? What difference would achieving these goals make to you? What is the cost of you staying where you are? How confident are you about achieving your goals? Who needs to be on your 'cheer squad' for you to be able to make the most of this journey (friends, colleagues, family members)? What needs to happen for you to be totally committed?
3. How do you intend to track your progress against this plan? What needs to be in place for you to sustain this journey?